Preparing Food For Your Freezer

Ice cream sundaes with fruits from your freezer make delectable desserts in a moment

Preparing Food For Your Freezer

Mary Norwak

WARD LOCK LIMITED · LONDON

Other Concorde Books

SIMPLE GREENHOUSE GARDENING
GARDENING FOR BEGINNERS
SIMPLE VEGETABLE GROWING
MAKING AND PLANNING
A SMALL GARDEN
PRACTICAL PRUNING
SHRUBS AND DECORATIVE
EVERGREENS
MRS BEETON'S FAVOURITE RECIPES
MRS BEETON'S CAKES AND BREADS
MRS BEETON'S PARTY DISHES
MRS BEETON'S SWEET DISHES
MRS BEETON'S FONDUE
AND CASSEROLE COOKERY
COLLECTING ENGLISH SILVER
COLLECTING ENGLISH ANTIQUES

Paperbound ISBN 0 7063 1214 7
Casebound ISBN 0 7063 1479 4

First published in Great Britain in 1974
by Ward Lock Limited, 116 Baker Street,
London, W1M 2BB

Reprinted 1975

Designed by Kaye Bellman

Text in Baskerville (169/312)

Printed and bound by Cox & Wyman Limited,
London, Fakenham and Reading

ACKNOWLEDGEMENTS

The Compiler and Publisher would like to thank the many individuals, manufacturers and institutions who have supplied specialist advice and pictures.

Special thanks are due to *Birds Eye Foods Limited* for the frontispiece photograph and others; to *Electrolux Limited* and *Philips Electrical Limited* for up-to-date, last-minute material; and to the *Dutch Dairy Bureau* and *Wall's (Ice Cream) Limited* for taking special photographs for this book. Cover photograph by courtesy of *Bacofoil Limited*.

Contents

Weights and Measures Used in this Book

Liquid measures

60 drops	1 teaspoon
3 teaspoons	1 tablespoon
4 tablespoons	$\frac{1}{2}$ gill
1 gill	$\frac{1}{4}$ pint
4 gills	1 pint
2 pints	1 quart
4 quarts	1 gallon

Homely solid measures

Spoons are British Standard teaspoons and tablespoons, which hold the amounts of liquid given above. They are measured with the contents levelled off, i.e. all the spoonfuls are level spoonfuls.

The cup is a British Standard measuring cup which holds 10 fluid oz or an Imperial $\frac{1}{2}$ pint.

Homely solid measures

Flour, sifted	3 tablespoons	1 oz
Castor or granulated sugar	2 tablespoons	$1\frac{1}{4}$ oz
Icing sugar, sifted	3 tablespoons	1 oz
Butter or margarine	2 tablespoons	$1\frac{1}{4}$ oz
Cornflour	2 tablespoons	1 oz
Granulated or powdered gelatine	4 teaspoons	$\frac{1}{2}$ oz
Golden syrup or treacle	1 tablespoon	1 oz
Flour, sifted	1 cup	5 oz
Castor or granulated sugar	1 cup	9 oz
Icing sugar, sifted	1 cup	5 oz
Butter or margarine	1 cup	9 oz
Cornflour	1 cup	8 oz
Golden syrup or treacle	1 cup	1 lb

Metric measures

Precise metric equivalents are not very useful. The weights are almost impossible to measure accurately, and are not used in ordinary cooking.

Schools use a 25-gram unit for 1 oz and for re-tested recipes. This means that they can use existing equipment. For instance, a 6-inch sandwich tin can be used for a 15-cm one, and a 7-inch tin for an 18-cm one. Yorkshire pudding using 100 grams plain flour fits into a 2×14 cm (8 in × $5\frac{1}{2}$ in) baking tin.

Introduction

Freezing is a quick method of preserving food safely. The activities of micro-organisms are slowed down as food approaches freezing point, and they become dormant at 0° F (−18° C). Most home freezers are designed to bring the food down to this temperature, and to maintain it for storage. Some home freezers can have their temperature reduced by a further 5° to 10° F for fast freezing. But really deep freezing is only possible commercially; commercial frozen-food stores are usually maintained at −20° F (−29° C).

The advantages of home freezing and bulk buying are now appreciated by more and more people, both town and country dwellers. Not only does a home-freezing system save you money through economic purchasing of seasonal or commercially frozen raw materials, but you also save time in shopping and by using a system of batch cookery.

Your home freezer can serve a dual purpose. It can combine the long-term storage of bulk raw materials which you have frozen at home or have bought, and the short-term storage of fresh foods, cooked dishes and leftovers which will have a quick turnover.

As for a fridge, every housewife knows the value of this piece of equipment in our busy modern age, when both delivery services and personal shopping time are limited. It is the most vital piece of kitchen equipment one can have, after a cooker.

Adaptable Freezing

Long-term storage is effective for the foods which you may buy cheaply from bulk suppliers; for farm and garden produce, and gluts of fresh food which are in season; also for special items, such as tropical fruits or rich cream, which you may get when on holiday, or which kind friends send you.

Short-term storage is a wonderful money-saver and way of varying meals by using cooked foods or leftovers. It is also useful if you do batch cookery of basic items such as roux or simple sauces: for items such as bread which you need regularly; you can buy them weekly or monthly: and for complete meals for sudden entertaining or emergency use.

Freezing is an easy process if you follow the basic instructions. These are not rigid rules but guide lines, showing how food can be kept well and retain flavour, colour and nutritive value. This book is designed for quick reference when preserving both raw materials and cooked foods. Types of food suitable for freezing are defined; but your individual requirements can only be assessed by experience, and by testing your favourite recipes under freezing conditions. The basic recipes included here are those which have proved successful in freezer storage and in subsequent cooking and eating.

The refrigerator is an invaluable aid to successful freezing. The freezer will function better if food is chilled in the refrigerator before being placed in the cabinet for freezing. The ice-making compartment of your refrigerator can also supply reserves of ice for rapidly chilling blanched vegetables and cooked dishes. Again, you can store large quantities of food temporarily in the refrigerator while the smaller recommended quantities are being frozen.

The refrigerator ice-making compartment can also be used for short-term storage of ice cream and other frozen products (see 'The Star System'). Frozen food should never be thawed quickly as rapid deterioration sets in, so the refrigerator is recommended for thawing almost all the items you freeze. The housewife who can assess her daily needs can transfer items from freezer to refrigerator storage first thing in the morning ready for later serving and further cooking if necessary.

THE STAR SYSTEM

The star markings on frozen-food compartments indicate the recommended storage times for individual packets of commercially frozen foods. These conform to British Standards Specification (No. 3739) and apply to the frozen-food compartments of domestic refrigerators.

* (one star) −6° C or 21° F stores bought frozen food for one week, and ice cream for one day.

** (two star) −12° C or 10° F stores bought frozen food for one month, and ice cream for two weeks.

*** (three star) −18° C or 0° F stores bought frozen food for three months, and ice cream for one month.

Three-star frozen-food compartments are normally capable of freezing down to 0° F within 24 hours small quantities of fresh or cooked food, according to individual refrigerator manufacturers' instructions.

A true food freezer however is capable of always operating at 0° F (−18° C) and is additionally capable of freezing unfrozen food to this temperature without any significant change in the temperature of the food already being stored. It can also store food for many months or even a year rather than weeks.

RUNNING COSTS

A freezer is not expensive to run. In average use, a 6 cubic food freezer uses .3 kW per cubic foot per 24 hours; 12 cubic foot uses .25 kW per cubic foot per 24 hours; 18 cubic foot uses .20 kW per 24 hours. The approximate cost is 1p per cubic foot per week. The size of machine and its design, the frequency and length of time of opening, and the temperature of food to be frozen can affect running costs.

INSURANCE OF CONTENTS

The contents of a freezer can be valuable, particularly if large quantities of meat or game are stored. Food stored in this way can be insured against loss at approximately £2 per £75 worth of food per annum.

Choosing a Freezer

The choice of a freezer will depend not only on the size of your family and the amount of your home produce but on the space available in kitchen or outhouse. Ideally, the freezer should be within easy reach of the cook, but excessive kitchen heat will put a heavy load on the cooling mechanism. Air must circulate freely round the freezer so that heat can be efficiently removed from the condenser. Dampness will damage both cabinet and motor.

Chest freezers are particularly suitable for locating in a garage or outhouse, and are excellent for bulk storage of such items as meat. Storage baskets make for tidiness, and help to divide food to be used soon from that which is kept for long-term storage. Very large commercial sizes are usually designed as chests, and represent considerable economy in purchasing as they are untaxed. It is important that a chest freezer has a magnetic lid seal and a self-balancing lid.

Upright freezers are very convenient for packing, with separate shelves for different types of food. There may be some slight intermittent rise in temperature in upright freezers as doors are often left open. Upright freezers have their weight concentrated in a small area, and it is important to check that the floor will take the weight of the freezer chosen.

Combination refrigerator freezers are very useful when space is limited as in a town house or flat. Normally, the freezer is on top of the refrigerator, but sometimes they are side by side. In either case the compartments are independent.

SPECIAL FEATURES TO LOOK FOR

Most freezers have a light which comes on when the electricity supply is connected and switched on; failure of the light means the power supply has been cut off and immediate investigation is necessary. Some freezers have a signal light connected to the thermostat which stays on as long as the cabinet temperature does not rise above a few degrees from the normal operating temperature.

Fast freezing compartments, switches and indicator lights are useful adjuncts to a freezer. Some freezers have a compartment divided by a panel or grid to keep still-unfrozen foods separate from stored foods while they are being processed. Some upright freezers have a shelf for fast freezing which is very useful for processing vegetables, cakes and pies which can be frozen before wrapping. The fast-freezing switch cuts out thermostatic control so that the motor runs continuously; heat is thus removed from unfrozen food as quickly as possible and the stored foods do not rise in temperature. The switch must be returned to normal running as soon as possible; sometimes the switch is wired in conjunction with an indicator light to show when the motor is running continuously.

Other useful additions to a freezer are storage baskets, which aid tidiness. Locks are useful to avoid pilfering if the freezer is stored in an outhouse; they also prevent children opening the freezer and leaving it open.

INSTALLING THE FREEZER

A newly installed freezer should be washed inside with warm water and dried thoroughly, then set at the recommended temperature for everyday use. The cabinet should be chilled for 12 hours before use.

CLEANING AND DEFROSTING

Defrosting is normally carried out when ice is $\frac{1}{4}$ inch thick. Manufacturers' instructions should be followed for occasional defrosting, but build-ups of ice may be removed with a plastic scraper. Sharp tools or wire brushes should not be used. For complete defrosting, food should be removed to a refrigerator or wrapped in layers of newspapers and blankets in a cold

A modern combination freezer

An upright freezer for small families

An up-to-date, well-stocked chest freezer seen from above

place. After defrosting, the freezer should be wiped completely dry and run at the coldest setting for 30 minutes before replacing food. The machine should then continue to run at the coldest setting for a further $2\frac{1}{2}$ hours before the switch is returned to normal setting.

The inside of the freezer is best cleaned with a solution of 1 quart water and 1 tablespoon bicarbonate of soda; the water should be lukewarm. Soap, detergent or caustic cleaners must not be used. The outside of the cabinet may be cleaned with warm soapy water and polished with enamel surface polish.

POWER FAILURE

When power fails, the freezer is best checked first for local causes. The switch may have been turned off by mistake, or the fuse in the plug may have 'blown'.

The cabinet should be left shut when power has failed, so that the cold temperature is retained. Properly packed food will last about 12 hours safely, although this depends on the load of food and on insulation. A fully packed freezer will maintain a low temperature for a long period.

Packing and Labelling

Freezing is not only an easy way of preserving both raw and cooked food, but it is also completely safe if the rules of hygiene are observed and food is correctly packed.

Good food will keep its quality and nutritive value in the freezer, but freezing cannot improve poor quality food.

BASIC FREEZING PROCEDURE

1 All food for freezing must be processed quickly, according to the instructions.

2 Food must be thoroughly chilled before being put in the freezer to avoid raising the temperature of food already stored.

3 Food must be carefully packed to exclude air, and should be labelled for identification. A simple record of the food in the freezer will aid meal planning and encourage you to maintain a steady turnover.

4 Food should be frozen quickly, preferably against the cold surfaces of the cabinet, and at the recommended low temperature.

5 Frozen cooked food must never be thawed and then refrozen. Raw materials should not be thawed and refrozen, but may be made into cooked dishes and frozen.

PORTIONS

Food should be prepared and packed in usable portions. Most people find it wise to prepare some large or family-sized packs and also a number of individual packs for use for single meals. Large packs of fruit and vegetables can be re-fastened after portions have been removed. A single portion of food will vary according to whether it is for a small child, a woman or a manual worker. Two people usually eat slightly less than two single portions when together.

PACKAGING MATERIALS

All packaging should be moisture and vapour proof, waterproof and greaseproof; durable and resistant to low temperatures; easily handled, economically stored and free from smell. Suitable materials are indicated for various groups of foods; individual packing methods are described where necessary.

Waxed tubs Waxed tubs are available with flush airtight lids and with screw-on tops. Waxed cartons are also made with fitted lids in square and rectangular shapes, and there are tall containers with tuck-in lids, and special ones with polythene liners which are suitable for food subject to leakage.

Rigid plastic containers Most branded plastic boxes are suitable for freezer storage. Those with flexible sides can be lightly pressed to aid removal of contents. Special Swedish freezer boxes are available which can be boiled for sterilization and which stack and save space.

Glass jars Screwtop preserving jars, bottles and honey jars may be used for freezing if tested for resistance to low temperature. Place an empty jar in a plastic bag in the freezer overnight; if it breaks, the bag will hold the pieces. Jars with 'shoulders' should not be used as this necessitates long thawing before the food can be turned out and used.

If using freezer-to-table ware, remember that it is a bad conductor of heat. This means that dishes are slow in heating but hold their heat for a long time. Allow extra time for water, stock or sauces to reach boiling point, but in all cookery remove from the heat a short while before you would do so in other pans. It is difficult to halt the cooking even after removal from heat; sauces tend, therefore, to solidify or curdle, eggs harden and seared meats burn.

Polythene Polythene bags are useful for almost all freezer food, and are available in a wide variety of sizes; they should be of the special heavy quality designed for low temperatures. Polythene sheeting is easy to handle for wrapping meat, poultry and pies, and its transparency makes quick identification easy.

PACKING FOR THE FREEZER

Beef

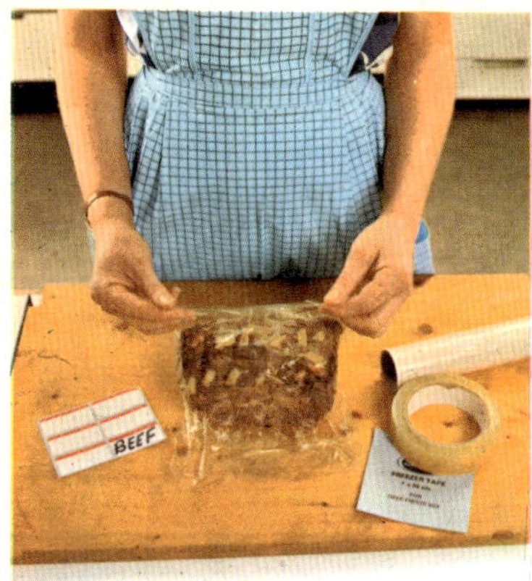

Chicken

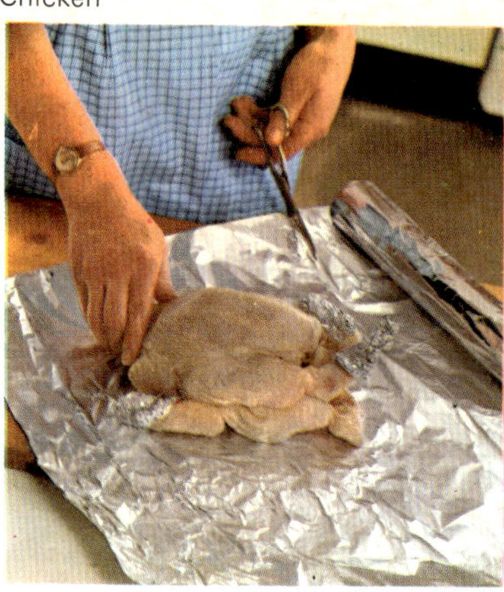

Vegetables

Fruit

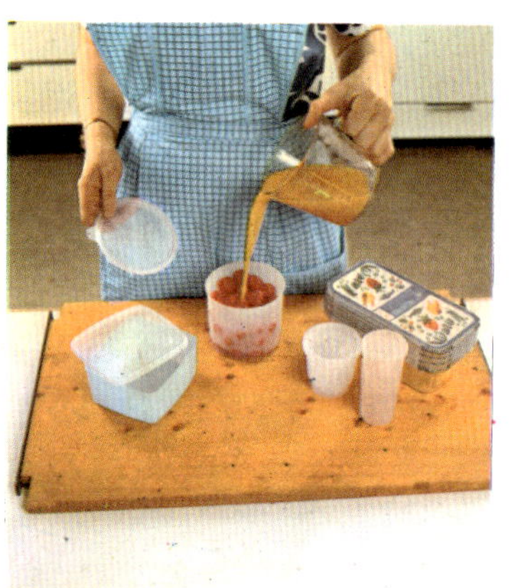

Foil and freezer paper Foil dishes are useful for dishes which are cooked before freezing and are later reheated, as one container may be used for all the processes. Heavy-duty foil sheeting is useful for overwrapping these dishes, and for packing both raw and cooked foods; it should be used with the dull side towards the food. Freezer paper is strong wrapping which is highly resistant to fat and grease, does not puncture easily, and has an uncoated outer surface on which labelling details may be written.

All types of container and sheet wrapping must be firmly

sealed. Bags can be closed with fasteners or heat-sealed with a special welding unit, or with a domestic iron used over thick paper. Special deep-freezing tape with gum which is resistant to low temperatures must be used for finishing sheet-wrapped packages and sealing containers with lids.

HEADSPACE AND AIR EXCLUSION

Containers with lids should be packed so that headspace from $\frac{1}{2}$ inch to 1 inch is left above the surface of the food to allow for expansion of contents, according to individual foods.

All sheet wrappings or bags must have the air pressed out so that the wrapping adheres closely to the food. When forming a parcel, the air can be pressed out with the hands. Air is most easily removed from bags by the insertion of a drinking straw at the closing, and by sucking the air out just before sealing.

PACKAGING

To avoid loss of quality, food should be carefully processed, packed, and then thawed or cooked quickly when needed. An enzyme is a type of protein which accelerates the chemical reactions in food. These reactions are slowed down by a freezing process, which is why freezing must be done quickly. Thawing speeds up enzymic reaction. It therefore encourages rapid deterioration, so that food is best thawed in a cold atmosphere such as a refrigerator, and must be eaten or cooked immediately after thawing.

Bad packaging causes a number of problems which will not render the food dangerous to eat, but which may cause an unattractive appearance, toughness and dryness, lack of flavour, or unpleasant mingling of flavours from different foods. Some of these are:

Dehydration and freezer burn Long storage and poor wrapping may result in the removal of moisture and juices, particularly from meat. This sometimes causes greyish-brown areas on food known as 'freezer burn'.

Oxidation and rancidity Oxygen from the air which penetrates wrappings reacts with fat cells in food to form chemicals which give meat and fish a bad taste and smell. Fried foods and fat meat and fish can suffer from this problem in the freezer. Salt accelerates this rancidity.

Broken packages and cross-flavourings Rough handling, sharp edges, brittle wrappings or overfilled containers may cause cracks or breakages which will result in dehydration or oxidation. This can also result in cross-flavouring with strongly flavoured foods, which may also spread smells and flavours if packages are not very strong or overwrapped.

Flabbiness Limp and flabby fruit and vegetables are caused by slow freezing, and sometimes by the choice of varieties unsuitable for freezing, which must be subject to trial and error. Suitable varieties are recommended in Chapter 4.

Ice crystals If too large a headspace is left on liquid foods in containers, a layer of ice crystals may form which will affect storage and flavour. Liquids can be shaken or stirred back into emulsion when heated or thawed. If the problem occurs in meat, fish, vegetables or fruit, it is usually because the food has been slow-frozen so that moisture in the cells has expanded and frozen and broken surrounding tissues. This results in juices and flavour being lost.

Suitable Packing Materials

The most commonly used packaging materials for various types of food are indicated thus *.

FOOD	WAXED OR RIGID PLASTIC CONTAINERS	FOIL CONTAINERS	FOIL SHEETING	POLYTHENE BAGS OR SHEETING
Fresh Meat			*	*
Fresh Poultry and Game			*	*
Fresh Fish			*	*
Cooked Meat and Fish Dishes	*	*	*	*
Fresh Vegetables	*			*
Fresh Vegetables (bline pack)	*			
Fresh Fruit (unsweetened or dry sugar pack)	*			*
Fresh Fruit (syrup pack)	*			
Butter, Margarine and Fats		*	*	*
Cheese			*	*
Milk and Cream	*			
Eggs	*	*		
Soups and Sauces	*	*	*	*
Bread, Cakes and Biscuits			*	*
Pastry and Pies		*	*	*
Desserts	*	*	*	*
Ice Cream	*		*	

Freezing and Thawing

Fruit

Home-grown fruit should be frozen on the day it is picked. Shop fruit such as pineapples or figs may be frozen when cheap and plentiful but should be handled in small quantities.

Fully flavoured fruit is the most successful. Bland fruit such as pears will appear satisfactory but have little flavour. Fruit should be of top quality in peak condition; unripe fruit will have a poor flavour and colour, although it can be preserved for future use in jam-making. Very ripe fruit should be stored as purée.

CLEANING AND GRADING

Fruit should be well washed in chilled water to avoid sogginess and loss of juice, then drained thoroughly and dried on absorbent paper. It must be handled gently when removing stems or stones, to avoid bruising and loss of juice. Copper, iron or galvanized ware should not be used in preparation since it will result in off-flavours. Silver implements should be used for fruit such as peaches.

Some fruit, such as strawberries, should be graded before packing to ensure even freezing and thawing. Fruit may be packed dry and unsweetened in a dry sugar pack, in an unsweetened wet pack, or in syrup.

UNSWEETENED DRY PACK

This can be used for fruit which will later be stewed or used for pies, or which is intended for those on a sugar-free diet. It is not suitable for fruit which discolours easily; sugar retards enzyme action which causes darkening. Fruit packed in this way should be cleaned and drained and packed into cartons or polythene bags.

UNSWEETENED WET PACK

Fruit may be packed in this way for people on a diet, or if the fruit itself is very sweet. The fruit can be crushed in its own juice or covered with water and lemon juice to prevent discoloration (juice of 1 lemon to 1½ pints water). It must be packed in leakproof containers. A sugar substitute or a sugar-free carbonated beverage may be added to the liquid.

DRY SUGAR PACK

Berries are particularly successful when frozen by this method, and it can be used for any fruit which is soft and juicy. Fruit may be crushed or sliced, or left whole if small. It may be mixed thoroughly with the sugar recommended and packed in cartons or polythene bags; or fruit may be packed in layers with sugar in cartons, leaving ½ inch headspace.

SYRUP PACK

Non-juicy fruits and those which discolour easily are best preserved in syrup. This is usually made with white sugar and water. (Honey flavours the fruit strongly; brown sugar affects the colour of the fruit.) Sugar syrup is made up in different proportions, and a medium syrup is normally used, since a heavy syrup tends to make fruit flabby.

Use a breakfast cup to measure quantities. Dissolve the sugar in boiling water, then cool it. The syrup is best chilled in a refrigerator overnight before use. The fruit must be packed in leakproof containers, and wholly covered with syrup, leaving headspace. A piece of cellophane pressed over the fruit and into the syrup before sealing will prevent discoloration.

Here is a table of syrups:

SUGAR	WATER	TYPE OF SYRUP	YIELD
1 cup	4 cups	20% very light syrup	5 cups
2 cups	4 cups	30% light syrup	5⅓ cups
3⅓ cups	4 cups	40% medium syrup	5½ cups
4¾ cups	4 cups	50% heavy syrup	6½ cups
7 cups	4 cups	60% very heavy syrup	7¾ cups
9 cups	4 cups	70% extra heavy syrup	8⅔ cups

PACKING AND LABELLING

Headspace must be left for all fruit in sugar or syrup, and for juice or purée. Allow ½ inch for all dry packs; ½ to 1 inch per pint for wide-topped wet packs; ¾ to 1 inch per pint for

As you can see, frozen apple slices make first-class pies and fillings

marrow-topped wet packs. Allow double headspace for quart containers.

Label fruit packs carefully, with ultimate use in mind if for pies or jam. Indicate type of pack, and amount of sweetening already included.

DISCOLORATION

In general, fruit containing a lot of Vitamin C darkens less easily than others, so that lemon juice or citric acid added to a sugar pack will help to arrest darkening. Use the juice of 1 lemon to $1\frac{1}{2}$ pints water, or 1 teaspoon citric acid to 1 lb sugar in a dry pack.

Apples, pears and peaches are particularly subject to discoloration. These fruits should be eaten quickly on thawing while a few ice crystals remain, as air reacts on the cells of fruit, causing darkening. For this reason, the fruit must be prepared quickly once the natural protection of skin or rind is broken.

Rapid thawing will help to prevent discoloration of fruit, and unsweetened frozen fruit may be put at once into hot syrup.

Fruit purée is subject to darkening owing to the amount of air forced through the sieve during preparation.

FRUIT PURÉE

Ripe fruit can be sieved and sweetened to freeze as purée. The fruit may be left raw, as with raspberries or strawberries. Other fruit can be cooked in the minimum of water or in its own juice (preferably in a covered dish in a low oven). Fruit purée will keep only 4 months.

FRUIT SYRUP

Any standard recipe can be used for Fruit Syrup*. This is best frozen in ice-cube trays, each frozen cube being wrapped in foil for storage; each should be big enough for one drink or serving of sauce.

FRUIT JUICE

Non-citrus fruit may be mashed with a silver fork, then covered with water (4 cups fruit to 1 cup water) and simmered for 10 minutes before straining through a jelly bag or cloth and cooled for freezing. Juice may be frozen unsweetened or sweetened, and is best prepared by the ice-cube method.

Apple juice can be made in the proportion of $\frac{1}{2}$ pint water to

2 lb apples or peelings may be simmered in water, using the same quantities. It must be sweetened as fermentation sets in quickly.
Citrus fruit for juice-making should be good quality and heavy in the hand for its size. Unpeeled fruit must be chilled in iced water before juice is extracted and strained.

SERVING FROZEN FRUIT

Raw frozen fruit is best served still slightly chilled and frosty. It is best thawed in the unopened container. Unsweetened fruit takes longer to thaw than sweet fruit; fruit in dry sugar thaws most quickly. Provision should be made for the amount of juice released from thawing fruit. Allow 6–8 hours for thawing a 1 lb fruit pack in syrup in the refrigerator; 2–4 hours at room temperature. Fruit will lose quality and flavour if left too long after thawing.

Fruit can be cooked immediately after removal from the freezer.

APPLES

Preparation and packing Peel, core and drop in cold water. Slice medium apples in twelfths, large apples in sixteenths. Slices may be blanched for 3 minutes and cooled before packing. Use:

1 Dry sugar pack, using ½ lb sugar to 2 lb fruit, with ½ inch headspace. Use containers, or pack in polythene bags.
2 40% syrup pack. Quarter-fill container with syrup, slice in apples, finishing with more syrup; cover with cellophane, leaving ½ inch headspace.

Thawing and serving Use frozen pie slices for pies and puddings, adjusting sweetening to taste.
Storage time 8–12 months.
Special notes Use firm crisp apples for pie slices; apples which fluff and burst may be frozen as purée or Apple Sauce*. Baked Apples* and Fruit Pies* may be ready-cooked before freezing.

APRICOTS

Preparation and packing Freeze unpeeled halves or peeled slices. Prepare in small quantities to avoid discoloration. **Half apricots** should be washed and stoned; drop in boiling water for ½ minute to prevent skins toughening, then chill in iced water. Use a dry sugar pack (4 oz sugar to 1 lb fruit) or 40% syrup. **Sliced apricots** should be peeled quickly and sliced

directly into containers holding a 40% syrup; they should be covered with cellophane, allowing ½ inch headspace.
Thawing and serving 3½ hours in pack at room temperature.
Storage time 12 months.
Special notes Lemon juice or citric acid can be added to give a better colour (see Discoloration). Very ripe fruit can be frozen as purée to serve as a sauce or for making ice cream.

AVOCADO PEARS

Preparation and packing Prepare as halves, slices or pulp. **Halves** should be rubbed with lemon juice, wrapped in foil, and stored in polythene bags. **Slices** must be dipped in lemon juice and frozen in waxed or rigid plastic containers. **Pulp** should be mashed, allowing 1 tablespoon lemon juice to each avocado, and should be packed in small containers.
Thawing and serving 2½ to 3 hours at room temperature. Use immediately when thawed. Mix pulp with onion, garlic or herbs for a dip or spread.
Storage time 2 months.
Special notes Subtlety of flavour is lost in freezing and fruit discolours very quickly. Pulp is more successful than halves or slices.

BANANAS

Preparation and packing Mash fruit in chilled bowl, mixing with 8 oz sugar to 3 breakfastcups banana pulp and 3 tablespoons lemon juice. Pack in small containers which can be used quickly.
Thawing and serving 6 hours in unopened container in refrigerator. Use for sandwiches or for bread and cakes.
Storage time 2 months.
Special notes There seems little reason to freeze bananas since supply and price vary little with the seasons. The fruit must be prepared very quickly as it discolours rapidly, and must also be used quickly on thawing. For children, Chocolate Covered Bananas* freeze well.

BLACKBERRIES

Preparation and packing Wash in chilled water and drain dry on absorbent paper. Pack whole berries in waxed or rigid plastic containers or polythene bags. As to sweetening:
1 Unsweetened berries may be fast frozen in a single layer on trays, then packed in bags.
2 Use a dry sugar pack, 8 oz sugar to 2 lb fruit, leaving

◀ Make this decorative flan with frozen apricots

headspace in containers, or packing in polythene bags.

3 Use a 50% syrup pack, leaving headspace.

Crushed berries may be sieved and sweetened, allowing 4 oz sugar to 1 pint crushed berries. Stir until dissolved, leaving ½ inch headspace.

Thawing and serving 3 hours at room temperature. Berries may be eaten raw with sugar, or cooked, or used in pies or puddings.

Storage time 1 year.

Special notes Dark glossy, fully ripe berries are best, preferably cultivated varieties. Berries with woody pips or green patches should be discarded.

BLUEBERRIES

Preparation and packing Wash in chilled water and drain thoroughly. The skins toughen on freezing, so crush fruit slightly first or hold over steam for 1 minute before cooling and packing. As to sweetening:

1 Unsweetened berries may be fast frozen in a single layer on trays, then packed in bags.

2 Use a dry sugar pack. 4 oz sugar to 4 breakfastcups berries is best, with berries slightly crushed and mixed with sugar until dissolved. Pack in containers or polythene bags.

3 Use a 50% syrup pack, leaving headspace.

Thawing and serving 3 hours room temperature. Fruit in syrup may be served cold; unsweetened or dry sugar packed berries may be cooked with water or used for pies.

Storage time 12 months.

CHERRIES

Preparation and packing Firm up cherries in chilled water for 1 hour; dry and remove stones which flavour fruit in freezing. Use glass or plastic containers as cherry juice acid tends to remain liquid and may leak through cardboard during storage.

1 Use a dry sugar pack. ½ lb sugar to 2 lb pitted cherries, packed in containers or polythene bags, is best for piemaking.

2 Use a 40% syrup pack, leaving headspace, for sweet cherries.

3 Use a 50% or 60% syrup pack, leaving headspace, for sour cherries.

Thawing and serving 3 hours at room temperature. Use sugared cherries for pies; syrup-packed cherries may be served cold.

Storage times 12 months.
Special notes Sweet and sour cherries freeze equally well, but red varieties do so better than black. Lemon juice or citric acid prevents darkening and helps flavour retention.

COCONUT

Preparation and packing Grate or shred fresh coconut, moisten with coconut milk, and pack into waxed or rigid plastic containers, or polythene bags. For sweet dishes, add 4 oz sugar to 4 breakfastcups of shredded coconut. Shredded coconut may also be toasted, cooled and packed.
Thawing and serving 2 hours at room temperature. Use for fruit salads or icings, or for curry dishes. It is best to drain off coconut milk immediately after thawing and before use.
Storage time 2 months.

CRAB APPLES

Preparation and packing Prepare as apple slices to use later for crab-apple jelly.
Storage time 12 months.

CRANBERRIES

Preparation and packing Discard shrivelled or soft berries. Wash in cold water and drain.

1 Unsweetened berries packed dry in bags or containers are the most useful, for later conversion into sauce or pies.
2 Purée berries by cooking gently in very little water until the skins pop; then sieve and add 8 oz sugar to each pint of purée. Allow $\frac{1}{2}$ inch headspace in containers.

Thawing and serving $3\frac{1}{2}$ hours at room temperature. Unsweetened berries can be cooked in water and sugar while still frozen.
Storage time 12 months.
Special notes Only firm, well-coloured glossy berries without mealiness should be used.

CURRANTS

Preparation and packing Strip fruit from stems with a fork, wash in chilled water and dry gently. As to sweetening:

1 Unsweetened berries may be packed dry in polythene bags for later use in jam-making.
2 Use a dry sugar pack, 8 oz sugar to 1 lb prepared berries; mix until almost dissolved, and pack in containers or suitable polythene bags.

3 Use a 40% syrup pack in containers.

Blackcurrants are also excellent if made into a purée, sweetened and packed into small containers to use for drinks, ices and puddings.

Thawing and serving $\frac{3}{4}$ hour at room temperature.

Storage time 12 months.

Special notes Black, red and white currants all freeze successfully by the same methods. *Boskoop Giant* and *Wellington* are good varieties of blackcurrants for freezing.

DAMSONS

Preparation and packing Wash fruit in chilled water, cut in half, remove stones, and use 50% syrup. The fruit is better as a purée, since the skins toughen during freezing and the stones flavour the fruit.

Thawing and serving $2\frac{1}{2}$ hours at room temperature.

Storage time 12 months.

DATES

Preparation and packing Wrap block dates in foil or polythene bags. Remove stones from dessert dates and pack in polythene bags or in waxed or rigid plastic containers.

Thawing and serving $\frac{1}{2}$ hour at room temperature. Serve as dessert, or use for cakes and puddings.

Storage time 12 months.

Special notes Dates stored in boxes dry out and develop off-flavours; so since they have a limited season, they are worth freezing.

FIGS

Preparation and packing Wash in chilled water, remove stems with a sharp knife, and handle carefully to avoid bruising.

1 Unsweetened figs may be frozen whole and peeled, or unpeeled, in polythene bags.
2 30% syrup pack may be used for peeled figs.
3 Dried dessert figs may be wrapped in foil or polythene bags.

Thawing and serving $1\frac{1}{2}$ hours at room temperature. Unsweetened figs may be eaten raw, or cooked in syrup.

Storage time 12 months.

Special notes Both green and purple figs can be frozen successfully. They should be fully ripe, soft and sweet, with small seeds and slightly shrivelled but unsplit skins.

Frozen strawberries give a party fillip to cream buns

GOOSEBERRIES

Preparation and packing Wash in chilled water and dry. As to sweetening:

1 Unsweetened fruit can be frozen in polythene bags without sweetening. For pies, fruit should be fully ripe. For jam, fruit may be frozen slightly under-ripe.

2 40% syrup may be used, but skins tend to toughen in storage.

3 Purée made by stewing fruit in very little water, sieving and sweetening to taste is useful for fools and mousses.

Thawing and serving $2\frac{1}{2}$ hours at room temperature. Fruit may be put into pies or cooked with sugar and water while still frozen. Purée should be used as soon as it is thawed.

Storage time 12 months.

Special notes The best variety for freezing is *Careless*.

GRAPEFRUIT

Preparation and packing Peel fruit, remove all pith and cut segments away from pith.

1 Use a dry sugar pack, 8 oz sugar to 2 breakfastcups segments, in waxed or rigid plastic containers.

2 Use a 50% syrup pack.

Thawing and serving $2\frac{1}{2}$ hours at room temperature.
Storage time 12 months.

GRAPES

Preparation and packing Seedless varieties can be packed whole; others should be skinned, pipped and halved. They are best packed in 30% syrup.
Thawing and serving $2\frac{1}{2}$ hours at room temperature.
Storage time 12 months.
Special notes Grapes should be firm, ripe, sweet and with tender skins. For decorative purposes, a perfect bunch of grapes may be frozen in a polythene bag and stored up to 2 weeks; the grapes look full and rich and taste excellent.

GREENGAGES

Preparation and packing Wash in chilled water and dry well. Cut in halves, removing stones, and pack in 40% syrup in waxed or rigid plastic containers.
Thawing and serving $2\frac{1}{2}$ hours at room temperature.
Storage time 12 months.
Special notes Skins tend to toughen during storage, and the stones flavour fruit, so an unsweetened dry pack is not recommended.

GUAVAS

Preparation and packing Wash fresh fruit, cook with a little water and purée. Cooking in pineapple juice improves flavour. Fruit can also be peeled, halved and cooked until tender, then packed in 30% syrup. Canned guavas can be packed in their own syrup.
Thawing and serving $1\frac{1}{2}$ hours at room temperature.
Storage time 12 months.

KUMQUATS

Preparation and packing Wrap whole fruit in foil, or cover with cold 50% syrup in waxed or rigid plastic containers.
Thawing and serving 2 hours at room temperature; use unsweetened fruit immediately after thawing.
Storage time 2 months if unsweetened; 12 months in syrup.

LEMONS AND LIMES

Preparation and packing Peel lemon or lime slices and freeze in 20% syrup in small packs.

Thawing and serving 1 hour at room temperature, to use as garnishes or in drinks.
Storage time 12 months.

LOGANBERRIES

Preparation and packing Treat as blackberries.
Thawing and serving 3 hours at room temperature. Fruit is particularly good for ices and mousses.
Storage time 12 months.

MANGOES

Preparation and packing Peel ripe fruit and slice into 50% cold syrup, having added 2 dessertspoons lemon juice to each quart syrup. Canned fruit can be frozen in syrup.
Thawing and serving $1\frac{1}{2}$ hours at room temperature.
Storage time 12 months.

MELONS

Preparation and packing Cut flesh in cubes or balls and toss in lemon juice before packing in 30% syrup.
Thawing and serving Thaw unopened in refrigerator and serve while still a little frosty.
Storage time 12 months.
Special notes Cantaloup and honey-dew melons and water-melons are all good frozen; but seeds make preparation of watermelon difficult.

NECTARINES

Preparation and packing Treat as peaches, peeling or not as desired.
Thawing and serving 3 hours in refrigerator.
Storage time 12 months.

ORANGES

Preparation and packing Oranges may be treated as grape-fruit in sections; but they are better in slices. Peel fruit and remove all pith, cutting flesh in $\frac{1}{4}$-inch slices. As to sweetening:

1 A dry sugar pack, using 8 oz sugar to 3 breakfastcups of orange pieces, can be packed in containers or polythene bags.
2 Use a 30% syrup in waxed or rigid plastic containers; covering with cellophane, leaving $\frac{1}{2}$ inch headspace.
3 Slices may be packed in slightly sweetened fresh orange juice.

Frozen apple slices used for fritters

Thawing and serving $2\frac{1}{2}$ hours at room temperature. Segments are most useful for breakfast, slices for other meals.
Storage time 12 months.
Special notes Navel oranges develop a bitter flavour when frozen.

PEACHES

Preparation and packing Deal with peaches one at a time as they discolour quickly. Peel, halve and slice, and brush with lemon juice. They are best peeled and stoned under cold running water, as boiling water used for skinning will cause them to soften and brown.

1 Use 40% syrup for halves or slices. Pack in waxed or rigid plastic containers and cover with cellophane, leaving $\frac{1}{2}$ inch headspace.

2 Purée peeled and stoned peaches, by crushing with a silver fork and mixing 1 tablespoon lemon juice and 4 oz sugar to each lb of fruit.

Thawing and serving Thaw slowly in refrigerator to prevent discoloration on exposure to the air. If to be used for cakes or with cream, use half-thawed so they will be ready by the time preparation of the dish is finished. Use purée for sauce or ice cream.
Storage time 12 months.

PEARS

Preparation and packing Peel and quarter, remove cores and dip pieces in lemon juice immediately. Poach pears in 30% syrup for 1½ minutes, drain and cool, and pack in cold syrup.
Thawing and serving 3 hours at room temperature.
Storage time 12 months.
Special notes Pears discolour badly during freezing, and do not retain their delicate flavour. The best pears to use are ripe, but not over-ripe.

PERSIMMONS

Preparation and packing Peel fully ripe fruit and freeze whole in 50% syrup; add 1 dessertspoon lemon juice to 1 quart syrup. Purée may be sweetened, allowing 1 breakfastcup sugar to 4 breakfastcups of purée. Whole unpeeled fruit may be wrapped in foil.
Thawing and serving 3 hours at room temperature. Use whole unpeeled fruit when barely thawed as it darkens and loses flavour when standing.
Storage time 2 months if raw; 12 months if in syrup or as purée.

PINEAPPLE

Preparation and packing Peel fruit and cut into slices or chunks. As to sweetening:

1 Unsweetened slices may be packed in boxes with double thickness of cellophane to keep slices separate.
2 Use a 30% syrup in waxed or rigid plastic containers, including any pineapple juice resulting from preparation; cover with cellophane, allowing ½ inch headspace.
3 Crush pineapple, allowing 4 oz sugar to 2 breakfastcups of prepared fruit.

Thawing and serving 3 hours at room temperature.
Storage time 12 months.
Special notes Pineapples, to freeze well, should be fully ripe with golden-yellow flesh.

PLUMS

Preparation and packing Treat as greengages. Dried prunes may be frozen as dates or figs.
Thawing and serving $2\frac{1}{2}$ hours at room temperature.
Storage time 12 months.

POMEGRANATES

Preparation and packing Cut fully ripe fruit in half, scoop out red juice sacs and pack them in 50% syrup in small containers. Juice may be extracted, sweetened to taste, and frozen in small containers or ice-cube trays, each frozen cube being wrapped in foil for storage.
Thawing and serving 3 hours at room temperature.
Storage time 12 months.

QUINCES

Preparation and packing Peel, core and slice and cook in boiling 20% syrup for 2 minutes, then pack in containers and cover with cold syrup. A better flavour is retained if the peel is simmered, with just enough water to cover it, and the juice of 1 orange and 1 lemon, until the peel is tender, this juice being used for making the syrup. As quinces take a long time to cook, they can be simmered until completely tender to save later preparation.
Thawing and serving 3 hours at room temperature.
Storage time 12 months.

RASPBERRIES

Preparation and packing Pick over fruit very carefully, discarding hard, seedy fruit. As to sweetening:

1 Unsweetened fruit may be packed in cartons or polythene bags.
2 A dry sugar pack, 4 oz sugar to 1 lb fruit, is suitable for cartons or polythene bags.
3 30% syrup may be poured over the fruit. Pack into containers, cover with cellophane and allow $\frac{1}{2}$ inch headspace.
4 Purée may be made by sieving fruit and sweetening with 4 oz sugar to each pint of purée. Pack in containers or in ice-cube trays, wrapping each frozen cube in foil for storage.

Thawing and serving 3 hours at room temperature. Purée may be used for sauce or drinks, or used as a basis for ice cream.
Storage time 12 months.
Special notes The best varieties for freezing are *Norfolk Giant* and *Lloyd George*.

RHUBARB

Preparation and packing Sticks should be washed in cold running water and trimmed to required length. For ease of packing, sticks can be blanched for 1 minute, which makes them limper and helps to retain colour and flavour. Pack in cartons or foil or polythene bags. As to sweetening:

1 A 40% syrup pack can be used for rhubarb cut in pieces. Pack in waxed or rigid plastic containers.

2 Stewed rhubarb may be sieved, sweetened and frozen as purée.

Thawing and serving 3½ hours at room temperature. Unsweetened sticks can be cut while still frozen and cooked in the usual way.

Storage time 12 months.

STRAWBERRIES

Preparation and packing Pick over fruit, removing husks, and using fully ripe, mature but firm strawberries. As to sweetening:

1 An unsweetened pack is recommended as strawberries are then less pulpy when thawed. They are best graded before packing. Pack in polythene bags.

2 A dry sugar pack, 4 oz sugar to 1 lb fruit, may be used with whole strawberries, or sliced or lightly crushed ones, packed in containers or polythene bags.

3 A 40% syrup can be used for whole or sliced fruit.

4 Strawberries may be sieved and sweetened to taste, then frozen as purée in small containers to use for ice cream or mousses.

Thawing and serving 1½ hours at room temperature. Unsweetened fruit may be sugared before thawing.

Storage time 12 months.

Special notes The best varieties for freezing are *Cambridge Vigour*, *Cambridge Favourite* and *Royal Sovereign*.

Vegetables

Home-grown vegetables freeze extremely well if young, tender and at the peak of perfection. Shop vegetables are rarely fresh enough to freeze, though imported delicacies such as peppers and aubergines are worth freezing for variety.

Vegetables should be prepared for freezing in small quantities, and are best prepared immediately after picking, preferably in the early morning. They must be blanched before processing, as the heat stops the chemical action of enzymes which affect quality, flavour and colour, and nutritional value during storage.

DO NOT FREEZE THESE VEGETABLES

Vegetables which do not retain their crispness such as salad greens and radishes should not be frozen. Tomatoes, celery and onions can be frozen for cooking, but not to serve raw. Cucumbers do not freeze well except in a vinegar pack.

CLEANING AND GRADING

Vegetables must be young and fresh. After thorough cleaning, they should be graded for size and cut if necessary. Vegetables must be fast frozen for best results, and should only be prepared in small quantities (normally 3 lb of food per cubic foot of freezer space can be frozen every 6 hours). Excess supplies can be stored in polythene bags in the refrigerator before freezing.

BLANCHING AND COOLING

Blanching is an essential process in vegetable preparation to retard enzyme action. Timing is important, as too little blanching will result in colour change and loss of nutritive value, while over-blanching results in loss of crispness and flavour. Blanching may be done by means of water or steam.

Water blanching Process only 1 lb of vegetables at a time so that water reaches all the vegetables and does not cool too quickly. Use a saucepan holding 8 pints of water, and a blancher, wire basket or muslin bag. Bring the water to the boil, immerse the vegetables in the container in the fast boiling water, cover tightly and keep the heat high. Calculate blanching time from when water returns to boiling point. Remove vegetables when done, and drain immediately. Water blanching is quicker than steam blanching, though there may be some loss of minerals and vitamins. It is preferable for leafy vegetables which may stick together in steam.

Steam blanching Put enough water in pan to prevent boiling dry. When water is boiling fast, put the container of vegetables into the steamer, cover tightly, and calculate the blanching time from when the steam escapes from the lid. Steam blanching takes half as long again as water blanching.

Cooling Cooling must be done very quickly and thoroughly, the vegetables being cool right through to the centre before packing. Chill in a large quantity of ice-chilled water, drain thoroughly and finish off by turning on to absorbent paper.

Vegetables which are not cooled quickly continue cooking in their own heat and go mushy.

PACKING

Bags or boxes may be used for packing, according to the quantity, the frailty of the vegetables and the importance of cheapness. Items such as artichokes or asparagus are best packed in boxes to avoid damage, but boxes are expensive to use for more common items such as peas or beans. Pack in small or large quantities according to ultimate use.

A dry pack is normally used for vegetables, but a brine pack helps to prevent some vegetables toughening in storage; this

Mixed vegetables diced in even slices for freezing

is particularly found in hard-water areas. Pack vegetables into rigid containers to within 1 inch of top and cover with brine (1 tablespoon salt to 1 pint water) leaving ½ inch headspace.

FAST FREEZING

Fast freezing is a method used to ensure vegetables are loose in their packs and can be shaken out in small quantities. If a freezer has no special equipment for this, vegetables can be frozen in a single layer on baking trays before packing in bags or boxes.

THAWING AND COOKING

Most vegetables should be cooked while still frozen for best results. If vegetables are in block form, break them up before heating so heat penetrates rapidly and evenly. Broccoli and spinach are the better for partial thawing. Corn on the cob requires special treatment. Completely thawed vegetables should be cooked immediately; 1 lb packets need 6 hours in a refrigerator for complete thawing, or 3 hours at room temperature.

Since frozen vegetables have already been partly cooked in blanching, they require less time for cooking than fresh vegetables. They should be cooked in very little water (about ¼ pint water to 1 lb vegetables depending on variety). The water should be fast boiling and the vegetables covered and simmered after boiling point is again reached. Vegetables may also be steamed, cooked in a double boiler, baked or cooked in butter.

Baking Vegetables should be separated and drained, put into a greased casserole with a knob of butter and seasoning, covered and cooked at 180° C, 350° F, Gas 4 for 30 minutes.

Cooking in butter A heavy pan should be used, and the vegetables cooked gently in melted butter until separate; they can then be cooked over moderate heat until tender.

MIXED VEGETABLES

Sometimes a mixture of vegetables is required, and these can be prepared and blanched separately, then packed together for freezing. Vegetables should be cut in even sizes for satisfactory cooking. The usual mixtures are of peas, beans, carrots and sweetcorn.

VEGETABLE PURÉE

Vegetables may be sieved, chilled and frozen in rigid containers leaving $\frac{1}{2}$ inch headspace. They are useful for subsequent use in soups. A purée for use as a vegetable should be reheated in a double boiler with butter and seasoning. Small quantities of purée may be frozen in ice-cube trays, each frozen cube being wrapped in foil for storage; these are particularly useful for babies and old people, one cube of purée providing an individual serving.

VEGETABLES IN SAUCE

There is little advantage in preparing and freezing vegetables in sauce, as cooked vegetables tend to lose flavour, texture and colour in the freezer. Better results are obtained by freezing vegetables after blanching, and preparing sauces to be frozen and used with the freshly cooked vegetables later.

If the two items must be put together, before freezing the vegetables should be slightly undercooked, and the complete dish cooled very quickly before freezing. It is best to reheat such a dish in a double boiler.

ARTICHOKES (GLOBE)

Preparation and packing Remove outer leaves and wash artichokes very thoroughly, trimming stalks and removing 'chokes'. Blanch six at a time in 4 quarts boiling water with 1 tablespoon lemon juice added, for 7 minutes. Cool in chilled water and drain upside down on absorbent paper. Pack in boxes, as polythene will tear.

Artichoke bottoms may be frozen for special dishes by removing all green leaves and centre flower, allowing 5 minutes for blanching.

Thawing and serving Plunge frozen artichokes in boiling water and boil for 5 minutes until leaves are tender and easily removed.

Storage time 12 months.

ASPARAGUS

Preparation and packing Remove woody portions and small scales and wash well. Sort and blanch each size separately. Cut into 6-inch lengths, and allow 2 minutes for small spears, 3 minutes for medium spears and 4 minutes for large spears. Cool and drain well. Pack, graded in sizes, in boxes lined with moisture–vapour-proof paper; or make up bundles with half the asparagus heads at each end, and wrap in freezer paper or foil.

Thawing and serving Put frozen asparagus into boiling

water and cook 5 minutes.
Storage time 9–12 months.

AUBERGINES (EGG PLANTS)

Preparation and packing Peel and cut into 1-inch slices, blanch 4 minutes, chill and dry in absorbent paper. Pack in cartons in layers separated by cellophane.

Cooked aubergines may well be frozen; they should be fried in deep fat after coating with thin batter, or egg and bread-crumbs, well drained and cooled before packing in layers, in cartons.

Thawing and serving Cook frozen aubergines in boiling water for 5 minutes. Heat frozen ready-cooked aubergines in a slow oven, or part-thaw and deep-fry.

Storage time Uncooked 12 months; cooked 1 month.

Special notes Aubergines will be rubbery unless they are frozen when mature and medium-sized, with tender seeds.

BAMBOO SHOOTS

Preparation and packing Portions of canned bamboo shoots can be put in small containers covered with liquid from the can, and frozen.

Thawing and serving Thaw at room temperature for 1 hour, drain and add to dishes.

Storage time 2 months.

BEANS (BROAD)

Preparation and packing Remove beans from shell, blanch for $1\frac{1}{2}$ minutes, cool and pack in cartons or polythene bags.

Thawing and serving Put frozen beans in boiling salted water and cook for 8 minutes.

Broad beans, shelled and bleached

Whole young carrots

Storage time 12 months.
Special notes Use small young beans with tender outer skins.

BEANS (FRENCH)
Preparation and packing Remove tops and tails, leaving small beans whole, and cutting bigger ones into 1-inch pieces. Blanch whole beans 3 minutes, cut beans 2 minutes. Cool and pack in polythene bags.
Thawing and serving Cook whole beans for 7 minutes in boiling salted water; cook cut beans for 5 minutes.
Storage time 12 minutes.

BEANS (RUNNER)
Preparation and packing Cut beans in pieces and blanch 2 minutes, cool and pack in polythene bags.
Thawing and serving Cook 7 minutes in boiling salted water.
Storage time 12 months.
Special notes If runner beans are shredded finely before freezing, the cooked result will be pulpy and tasteless.

BEETROOT
Preparation and packing Only very young beetroot, under 3 inches in diameter are suitable for freezing. Cook in boiling water until tender, putting larger beetroot in water first and adding the remainder in graduated sizes at 10-minute intervals. Cool quickly in running water, rub off skins and pack in cartons. Beetroot under 1 inch diameter may be frozen whole; large ones should be sliced or diced.

Thawing and serving Thaw in cartons in refrigerator for 2 hours, drain and add dressing.
Storage time 6–8 months.
Special notes Short blanching and long storage make beetroot rubbery, so complete cooking is essential.

BROCCOLI
Preparation and packing Compact heads with tender stalks not more than 1 inch thick should be used, and these heads should be uniformly green. Trim woody stems and take off outer leaves. Wash well and soak in salt water (2 teaspoons salt to 8 pints water) to clear out insects, for 30 minutes. Wash in fresh water. Cut into sprigs and blanch 3 minutes for thin stems, 4 minutes for medium stems, 5 minutes for thick stems. Pack into bags or boxes, with half the heads at each end.
Thawing and serving Plunge frozen heads into boiling water and cook for 8 minutes.
Storage time 12 months.

BRUSSELS SPROUTS
Preparation and packing Use small compact heads and grade well before blanching. Clean and wash well. Blanch 3 minutes for small sprouts, 4 minutes for medium sprouts; cool and pack in cartons or bags.
Thawing and serving Cook frozen sprouts for 8 minutes in boiling water.
Storage time 12 months.

CABBAGE (GREEN AND RED)
Preparation and packing Use young crisp cabbage. Wash thoroughly and shred finely. Blanch $1\frac{1}{2}$ minutes, and pack in polythene bags.
Thawing and serving Cook for 8 minutes in boiling salted water.
Storage time 6 months.
Special notes Frozen cabbage should not be used raw for salads.

CARROTS
Preparation and packing Use very young carrots, wash thoroughly and scrape. They may be packed whole, sliced or diced. Blanch whole small carrots (or cut carrots) for 3 minutes. Pack in cartons or polythene bags, leaving $\frac{1}{2}$ inch headspace in cartons.

Thawing and serving Cook frozen carrots for 8 minutes in boiling water.
Storage time 12 months.

CAULIFLOWER

Preparation and packing Heads should be firm and compact with close white flowers. Wash and break into small sprigs. Add the juice of a lemon to blanching water to keep cauliflower white. Blanch 3 minutes, cool, and pack in lined boxes or polythene bags.
Thawing and serving Cook for 10 minutes in boiling water.
Storage time 6 months.

CELERY

Preparation and packing Use crisp young stalks, removing any strings. Scrub well and remove dirt under running water. Cut in 1-inch lengths and blanch for 3 minutes. Drain, cool, and pack in polythene bags. Celery may also be packed in rigid containers covered with flavoured water used for blanching, leaving $\frac{1}{2}$ inch headspace.
Thawing and serving Add to stews or soups, or cook as a vegetable, using its own liquid if frozen by this method.
Storage time 6 months.
Special notes Since celery must be blanched for freezing, it cannot then be used for raw salads and snacks, but it is useful for cooked dishes.

CHESTNUTS

Preparation and packing Cover chestnuts in shells with water and bring to the boil. Drain and peel off shell and pack in containers or polythene bags. It is possible to pack the chestnuts in shells, but it becomes extremely difficult to shell them after thawing.
Thawing and serving Plunge frozen chestnuts into boiling water or milk to cook, according to recipe being followed.
Storage time 6 months.

CORN ON THE COB

Preparation and packing Corn must be fresh and tender. It may be frozen as cobs or kernels.
Cobs should be graded when leaves and silk threads are removed, and stems cut short. They should not be starchy or over-ripe, nor have shrunken or under-sized kernels. Blanch 4 minutes for small cobs, 6 minutes for medium cobs, and 8

minutes for large cobs. Cool and dry, and pack individually in freezer paper or foil. Freeze immediately in coldest part of freezer, then pack in bags.

Kernels can be scraped from blanched cobs and packed in cartons leaving $\frac{1}{2}$ inch headspace.

Thawing and serving Correct cooking after freezing is particularly important with corn.

1 Put frozen corn in enough cold water to cover it completely. Put on high heat, bring to a fast boil and simmer 5 minutes.
2 Thaw in wrappings in refrigerator, plunge in boiling water and cook 10 minutes.
3 Preheat oven to 180° C, 350° F, Gas 4 and roast for 20 minutes, or wrap in foil to roast on a barbecue, turning frequently.

Storage time 12 months.

CUCUMBER

Preparation and packing Mix equal quantities of white

Corn on the Cob

vinegar and water, and season with $\frac{1}{2}$ teaspoon sugar and $\frac{1}{4}$ teaspoon black pepper to each pint of liquid. Fill rigid plastic containers with liquid, and slice in the cucumber thinly, leaving 1 inch space.
Thawing and serving Thaw in covered container in the refrigerator; drain and season with salt.
Storage time 2 months.
Special notes Frozen cucumber is not usually considered very satisfactory, but this method is good for those who like cucumber dressed with vinegar.

FENNEL

Preparation and packing Prepare as celery, retaining blanching liquid for packing. Blanch 3 minutes.
Thawing and serving Simmer frozen fennel in blanching water or stock for 30 minutes. Slip hard cores from centres of roots when cooked.
Storage time 6 months.

HERBS

Preparation and packing Wash herbs thoroughly, trim from stems, and cut very finely. Put into ice-cube trays, topping up with water and freeze. Wrap frozen cubes in foil and pack in polythene bags for easy storage. *Parsley*, *mint* and *chives* freeze most successfully.
Thawing and serving Thaw at room temperature for use in sandwich fillings; add frozen cubes to sauces, soups or stews.
Storage time 6 months.
Special notes Sprigs of herbs become limp on thawing, so are not suitable for freezing as garnishes. The flavour of frozen herbs is good but not strong; colour retention is good.

KALE

Preparation and packing Use young, tender, tightly curled kale, discarding dry or tough leaves. Remove leaves from stems and blanch 1 minute. Cool, drain, and chop if liked. Pack tighly into bags or containers leaving $\frac{1}{2}$ inch headspace.
Thawing and serving Cook frozen kale in boiling water for 8 minutes.
Storage time 6 months.

KOHLRABI

Preparation and packing Use mild-flavoured kohlrabi which is not too large but is young and tender. Trim, wash and

peel, leaving small ones whole, and dicing large ones. Blanch whole vegetables for 3 minutes; diced for 2 minutes. Cool and pack in polythene bags or containers, leaving $\frac{1}{2}$ inch headspace for diced vegetables.
Thawing and serving Cook frozen kohlrabi for 10 minutes in boiling water.
Storage time 12 months.

MARROW

Preparation and packing Young marrows or courgettes can be frozen unpeeled, cut in $\frac{1}{2}$-inch slices and blanched for 3 minutes before packing in cartons with $\frac{1}{2}$ inch headspace. Older vegetables should be peeled and seeded, cooked until soft, then mashed and packed.
Thawing and serving Cook sliced marrows by frying in oil and seasoning well with salt and pepper. Reheat cooked mashed marrow in a double boiler with butter and plenty of seasoning.
Storage time 6 months.

MUSHROOMS

Preparation and packing Use only very fresh mushrooms, wiping clean but not peeling. Mushrooms larger than 1 inch diameter should be sliced. The stems should be trimmed off, and can then be frozen separately. Blanch $1\frac{1}{2}$ minutes in water, adding 1 tablespoon lemon juice to 6 pints water. Blanch stems separately for $1\frac{1}{2}$ minutes. Pack cups down in containers, leaving $\frac{1}{2}$ inch headspace.
Cooked mushrooms freeze excellently if graded into sizes and cooked gently for 5 minutes, allowing 6 tablespoons butter to 1 lb mushrooms. Cool quickly, and take off excess fat before packing.
Thawing and serving Thaw uncooked mushrooms in a covered container in the refrigerator, then cook in butter. Add frozen cooked mushrooms to soups, stews or other dishes as required by recipe.
Storage time 3 months.

ONIONS

Preparation and packing Onions may be frozen raw for use in salads, or cooked.
Raw onions can be peeled, chopped and packed in small containers for later cooking. They may also be cut in $\frac{1}{4}$-inch

slices and wrapped in freezer paper or foil, with slices divided by cellophane. Packages should be overwrapped to prevent the onions flavouring other foods in the freezer.
Prepared onions may be chopped or sliced, blanched 2 minutes, then chilled, drained and packed, with overwrapping. Small whole onions should be blanched 4 minutes.
Thawing and serving Thaw raw onions on absorbent paper in the refrigerator, and serve while still frosty in salads. Add raw or prepared onions to cooked dishes according to recipe followed.
Storage time 2 months.

PARSNIPS

Preparation and packing Trim and peel young parsnips and cut into narrow strips or dice about $\frac{1}{2}$ inch thickness. Blanch 2 minutes and pack in containers or polythene bags.
Thawing and serving Cook frozen parsnips in boiling water for 15 minutes.
Storage time 12 months.

PEAS

Preparation and packing Use young sweet peas which are not old or starchy. Shell, and blanch 1 minute, lifting blanching basket in and out of water to distribute heat evenly through layers of peas. Chill quickly and pack in polythene bags or rigid containers.
Edible pod peas should be flat and tender. Wash well, and remove both ends and any strings. Blanch $\frac{1}{2}$ minute in small quantities so peas remain crisp.
Thawing and serving Cook frozen shelled peas or frozen edible pods for 7 minutes in boiling water.
Storage time 12 months.

PEPPERS (GREEN AND RED)

Preparation and packing Freeze green and red peppers separately or in mixed packages. They may be frozen in halves for stuffing, or in slices for use in stews or sauces. Wash weli, cut off stems and caps, remove seeds and membranes. Blanch halves 3 minutes, slices 2 minutes. Pack in rigid containers or polythene bags.
Roast red peppers may be prepared by grilling under a high heat until skin is charred, then plunging into cold water and rubbing off skins. Remove caps and seeds, and pack tightly

New potatoes

in rigid containers in salt solution (1 tablespoon salt to 1 pint water) leaving 1 inch headspace.

Canned peppers which are left unused may be frozen in small containers in liquid from the can.

Thawing and serving Thaw uncooked peppers for $1\frac{1}{2}$ hours at room temperature before using. Roasted peppers should be thawed in their containers, in the salt solution, then drained and dressed with olive oil and seasoning. Canned peppers should be thawed in their containers at room temperature and should be used immediately after thawing.

Storage time 12 months; canned peppers 2 months.

POTATOES

Preparation and packing Potatoes are best frozen when small and new, or in cooked form as chips, croquettes, Baked Potatoes* or Duchesse Potatoes*.

New potatoes should be scraped and washed, blanched 4 minutes, cooled and packed in polythene bags. They may also be slightly undercooked, drained, tossed in butter, cooled quickly and packed.

Mashed potatoes can be made with butter and hot milk, and frozen in bags or waxed cartons. The same mixture can

be used for **Croquettes** to be fried, drained and cooled before packing.
Chips should be cooked in clean odour-free fat, drained on paper, cooled and packed in polythene bags.
Thawing and serving Cook **new potatoes** in boiling water for 15 minutes; **buttered new potatoes** can be reheated by plunging the freezing bag in boiling water, removing from heat and leaving for about 10 minutes.
Mashed potatoes should be reheated in a double boiler, or can be slightly thawed, then spread on meat or fish cooked in the oven. **Croquettes** should be thawed for 2 hours at room temperature before heating at 180° C, 350° F, Gas 4 for 20 minutes.
Chips may be heated in a frying pan with a little hot fat, or on a baking tray at 150° C, 300° F, Gas 2 for 12 minutes.
Storage time New potatoes 12 months; cooked potatoes 3 months.

PUMPKIN

Preparation and packing Treat as cooked marrow.
Thawing and serving Reheat in double boiler with butter and seasoning as a vegetable; or thaw at room temperature for 2 hours to use as pie filling.
Storage time 6 months.

SPINACH

Preparation and packing Use young tender spinach, remove stems and discoloured or bruised leaves. Wash very well and blanch 2 minutes, shaking blanching basket so that leaves separate. Cool quickly and press out excess moisture. Pack in rigid containers, leaving ½ inch headspace, or in polythene bags.
Thawing and serving Melt a little butter in heavy pan, and cook frozen spinach for 7 minutes.
Storage time 12 months.

TOMATOES

Preparation and packing Tomatoes should not be frozen for salad use, but are good for cooking. They are most usefully frozen in the form of pulp, but can also be frozen whole or as juice.
Whole tomatoes should be wiped clean, the stems removed, and the tomatoes packed in usable quantities in polythene bags.

Tomato pulp is best prepared by skinning and coring tomatoes, then simmering them in their own juice for 5 minutes until soft. Sieve, cool and pack in small containers.
Tomato juice is made from cored and quartered ripe tomatoes simmered with a lid on for 10 minutes. Put through muslin, cool and pack into cartons leaving 1 inch headspace.
Thawing and serving Thaw **whole tomatoes** at room temperature for 2 hours before cooking. Thaw **purée** in container at room temperature for 2 hours before using, or turn frozen purée into soup or stew as required in recipe being followed. Thaw **juice** in its container in the refrigerator and serve a little frosty, seasoned to taste.
Storage time Whole tomatoes 10–12 months; purée 12 months; juice 12 months.

TURNIPS

Preparation and packing Use small, young, mild turnips. Trim and peel, and cut into ½-inch dice. Blanch 2½ minutes, cool, and pack in rigid containers.
Mashed turnips can be made by cooking turnips until tender, draining and mashing, then freezing in rigid containers leaving ½ inch headspace.
Thawing and serving Cook frozen turnips in boiling water for 10 minutes. Heat mashed turnips in a double boiler with butter and seasoning.
Storage time 12 months; mashed turnips 3 months.

Meat, Poultry, Game, Fish and Shellfish

Both money and shopping time can be saved by storing meat, poultry and game, both fresh and cooked, in the freezer. You can buy meat in bulk either from a local butcher or a specialist supplier. But do remember that the purchase of a whole carcass may not be an economy if some cuts are hardly ever used in your household; the saving on legs, shoulders or loins may be offset by the quantities of cheaper cuts which are not popular in your family, and which take time and trouble to prepare. So you will be wise to assess your needs carefully, and invest in bulk supplies of joints, individual steaks and chops or cheaper meat prepared for pies and stews.

Many butchers feel that meat should be prepared only by deep freezing, which is not possible under home conditions, but the home freezer can certainly be used if care is taken, and if only small quantities are prepared at a time.

QUALITY OF MEAT

Meat for freezing must be of high quality, and must have been hung for the required time. Nothing will improve the texture or flavour of poor meat, though tender meat can become a little more tender in storage. Pork and veal are normally only chilled before freezing; beef is aged for eight to ten days, and lamb for five to seven days.

PREPARATION FOR FREEZING

Meat for freezing should if possible be boned. Remove all surplus fat, and prepare the meat in the form in which it is to be cooked. If a lot of meat is to be prepared at one time, begin by freezing offal, then pork, then veal and lamb, and finally beef which will keep best under normal refrigeration if delays occur. No more than 4 lb of meat for each cubic foot of freezer space should be frozen at one time.

Bad packing is responsible for many of the faults which cause criticism of frozen meat. Wrapping should be strong so that oxygen does not penetrate and affect the fat which causes rancidity (pork is particularly subject to this problem). Over-wrapping will prevent damage to packages, and bones should be padded with greaseproof paper to prevent them piercing the wrappings. Air must be completely excluded so that the freezer wrapping stays close to the meat and prevents drying out.

THAWING FROZEN MEAT

Experiments continue on cooking meat direct from the freezer, but so far the methods used do not produce perfect results. Slow thawing all over is required, and meat is best thawed in its wrappings in a refrigerator; this helps the meat retain its juiciness. Thin cuts of meat and minced meat toughen when cooked while frozen. (Commercially frozen meat is processed.) Offal must be completely thawed.

Allow 5 hours per lb in a refrigerator and 2 hours per lb at room temperature for thawing meat; for offal, sausages and mince, allow 3 hours in a refrigerator and 1½ hours at room temperature. If you have to cook meat from the frozen state, unthawed large cuts will take 1½ times as long as fresh ones to cook, and smaller thin ones will take 1¼ times as long.

COOKING FROZEN MEAT

Meat should be cooked as soon as it has thawed, while it is still cold, to prevent loss of juices. The same methods as for

Frying chops after thawing

cooking fresh meat should be used. Chops and steaks cook best in a thick frying pan lightly oiled, starting with gentle heat on both sides before browning more quickly. Joints are best cooked by a slow-oven method if still chilled 150° C, 300° F, Gas 2 for beef and lamb; 180° C, 350° F, Gas 4 for pork.

JOINTS

Preparation and packing Prepare beef, lamb, mutton, pork or veal in the form in which it is ready to cook. Remove bones if possible, trim surplus fat and tie joint into shape. Wipe meat and pad sharp bones. Wrap and seal in freezer paper, heavy-duty foil or polythene, excluding air, and overwrap.
Thawing and serving Thaw in wrappings in refrigerator, allowing 5 hours per lb. Prepare to chosen recipe, using slow-oven method.
Storage time Beef 10–12 months; lamb, mutton and veal 6–8 months; pork 4 months.

STEAKS AND CHOPS

Preparation and packing Package in quantities which can be used at one time. Individual portions may be packed then stored in quantity in polythene bags for easy handling. Separate individual pieces of meat with cellophane or greaseproof paper and wrap in freezer paper, foil or polythene.
Thawing and serving Thaw in wrappings in the refrigerator. Steaks and chops are best cooked gently in a well-oiled heavy

pan, with a higher heat for final browning.
Storage time 4–12 months according to type of meat.

MINCED AND CUBED MEAT

Preparation and packing Mince of good quality, without fat, should be packed into cartons or polythene bags, excluding air. The addition of salt shortens its storage life. Mince may also be packed in the form of shaped patties, to use as hamburgers; they should be separated by sheets of greaseproof paper or cellophane, and packed in cartons or bags.
Cubed meat to be used for pies or stews should be trimmed of fat and pressed tightly into cartons or polythene bags in usable quantities.
Thawing and serving Thaw in wrappings in refrigerator for 3 hours, or at room temperature for $1\frac{1}{2}$ hours. If the meat is needed quickly, it may be placed in boiling stock and stirred well to help separation.
Storage time 2 months.

OFFAL

Preparation and packing Hearts, **liver**, **kidneys**, **sweetbreads** and **tongue** should be washed thoroughly and dried, and all blood vessels and pipes should be removed. Wrap in cellophane or polythene, and put into cartons or polythene bags. **Liver** may be frozen whole or sliced, with the slices

Thawed meat ready for roasting

separated by greaseproof paper or cellophane. **Tripe**, cut in 1 inch squares, may be packed in polythene bags.
Thawing and serving Thaw completely in wrappings for 3 hours in refrigerator or 1½ hours at room temperature, and prepare to chosen recipe.
Storage time 2 months.
Special notes Offal is prone to developing off-flavours, so must be carefully packaged and used in minimum time.

SAUSAGES AND SAUSAGE MEAT

Preparation and packing Omit salt in preparation as this shortens the freezer life. Pack tightly in freezer paper, foil or polythene.
Thawing and serving Sausages can be cooked in their frozen state. Thaw sausage meat in wrappings in refrigerator for 2 hours.
Storage time 1 month.

COOKED COLD MEAT

Preparation and packing Cut in slices and separate with cellophane or greaseproof paper. Slices should be ¼ inch thick and tightly packed to avoid drying. Pack in bags or cartons. Meat can also be packed in gravy thickened with cornflour. Both meat and gravy must be cold before combining and packing in foil dishes.
Thawing and serving Thaw slices for 3 hours in refrigerator, in wrappings, then separate and put on absorbent paper to remove moisture.

For meat and gravy, put the freezer foil dish with a foil lid on it into oven and heat at 180° C, 350° F, Gas 4 for 25 minutes.
Storage time Meat slices 2 months; meat in gravy 1 month.
Special notes Ham and pork lose colour when stored in slices without gravy. Whole cooked joints, steaks or chops tend to toughen on reheating, and the outer surface often develops off-flavours. Fried meats tend to toughness, dryness and rancidity when frozen.

GALANTINES AND MEAT LOAVES

Preparation and packing Make your usual recipe for Galantine* or Meat Loaf*, using a loaf tin. If the dish is to be cooked after freezing, line the tin with foil, freeze the mixture, then form the foil into a parcel for storage. Cooked galantines or meat loaves can be packed in freezer paper or foil; or they may be packed in slices separated by cellophane or grease-

proof paper, wrapped in freezer paper or foil.
Thawing and serving Thaw cooked dishes in the refrigerator, in wrappings, overnight. A meat loaf to serve as a hot dish may be reheated, without thawing, at 180° C, 350° F, Gas 4 for 45 minutes; an uncooked meat loaf will need 1 hour 40 minutes.
Storage time 1 month.

CASSEROLES AND STEWS

Preparation and packing Use your favourite recipe, including any containing wine, but keep the fat content low. Slightly undercook vegetables to avoid softness. Do not add potatoes, rice or other starch. Use cornflour for thickening to prevent curdling. Be sure meat is covered with liquid to prevent drying out.

Pack in freezer-to-oven containers, in cartons, or in a foil-lined casserole from which the foil package can be removed for storage.
Thawing and serving Heat in a double boiler over direct heat if curdling is not likely to occur; or heat in the original container in a moderate oven 180° C, 350° F, Gas 4 for 45 minutes.
Storage time 1 month.
Special notes For practical purposes, it is useful to double a normal family recipe, using half the quantity immediately and freezing the remainder.

COTTAGE PIE

Preparation and packing Make from fresh or cooked meat, and make meat moist with plenty of stock or gravy. Cool completely and put in a foil container. Prepare mashed potatoes and cool completely. Spread the potatoes on the meat. Cover the dish with foil or put the container into a polythene bag for storage.
Thawing and serving Heat frozen cottage pie at 200° C, 400° F, Gas 6 for 35 minutes until the potatoes are crisp and golden.
Storage time 1 month.

MEAT BALLS

Preparation and packing Prepare the standard recipe for Meat Balls*. Pack in polythene bags, or in containers, with layers divided by greaseproof paper or cellophane.
Thawing and serving Do not thaw, but fry quickly in hot

Pack meat in a gelatine closely, since aspics go cloudy on freezing. Top with clear aspic while thawing

fat, or heat in Tomato* or Brown* sauce.
Storage time 1 month.

HAM AND BACON

Packing and preparation Better stored in the piece than sliced. Pack in freezer paper, foil or polythene, and overwrap. Sliced bacon should be packed in the same way.
Thawing and serving Thaw in wrappings, in the refrigerator, before using in normal way.
Storage time 3 months in piece; 3 weeks if in slices.
Special notes Cured and smoked meats are best stored in a cool atmosphere, free from flies and dust. There is little advantage in freezing them as their storage life is limited, and salt tends to cause rancidity in fat meats during freezing.

PREPARING AND PACKING POULTRY

Poultry should be in perfect condition, starved for 24 hours before killing, hung and bled well. Skin damage when plucking should be avoided, and scalding will increase the chance of

A thawed roasted bird with stuffing balls fried before freezing

freezer burn. A bird should be cooled in a refrigerator for 12 hours before freezing, and be drawn and completely clean.

Whole birds should be trussed neatly, or it may be more convenient to freeze halves or joints. Bones should be padded with greaseproof paper to avoid damage to packaging. Joints should be divided by cellophane for easy separation. Air must be completely removed so that the wrapping fits closely to the bird. Giblets and livers should be packaged separately, and stuffing should be omitted.

THAWING POULTRY

Poultry should be thawed in its unopened freezer wrapping, and this is best done in the refrigerator to give slow, even thawing. Flavour will be better if bird is completely thawed before cooking. A 4–5 lb chicken will thaw overnight in a refrigerator or in 4 hours at room temperature. A turkey of 9 lb will take 36 hours to thaw, while a large bird may take as much as three days; for practical purposes a cool room is generally the best place for thawing such a large bird. A thawed bird may be stored up to 24 hours in a refrigerator, but no more.

CHICKENS, DUCKS, GEESE AND TURKEYS

Preparation and packing Poultry should be cooled for 12 hours in the refrigerator before packing. Truss whole birds, or joint neatly. Pad bones with greaseproof paper. Divide joints with layers of greaseproof paper or cellophane. Pack in polythene bags, removing all air. Omit giblets, liver and stuffing. Remove oil glands from geese and ducks.
Thawing and serving Thaw, in unopened wrappings, in the refrigerator. Allow a 4–5 lb chicken to thaw overnight in the refrigerator; if necessary, thaw it in 4 hours at room temperature. Allow 36 hours for a 9 lb turkey and up to 3 days for a larger bird. Cook by normal methods.
Storage time Whole chickens and turkeys 8–12 months; chicken and turkey pieces 6–10 months; geese and ducks 6–8 months.

GIBLETS

Preparation and packing Clean, wash, dry and chill, and pack in polythene bags, excluding air. For quicker preparation after freezing, giblets may be cooked and frozen in stock in leakproof containers.

Thawing and serving Thaw in wrappings for 2 hours in refrigerator, and use for soups, stews or pies.
Storage time 2 months uncooked; 1 month cooked.

POULTRY LIVERS

Preparation and packing Clean, wash, dry and chill, and pack in polythene bags, excluding air.
Thawing and serving Thaw in wrappings for 2 hours in the refrigerator, and use for omelettes, risotto or pâté.
Storage time 2 months.

STUFFING

Preparation and packing Prepare Basic Poultry Stuffing*, keeping it very cold. Pack in cartons or polythene bags. The mixture may be formed into balls, deep-fried, cooled and packed in cartons.
Thawing and serving Thaw the stuffing in its wrappings in the refrigerator for 2 hours before using it to stuff bird. If cooked, put it in roasting tin with poultry, or in casserole 10 minutes before serving time.
Storage time 1 month.

COOKED POULTRY

Preparation and packing Prepare in slices, or in gravy or sauce, as for Cooked Cold Meat. Chicken pieces can be prepared as Fried Chicken* and packed individually, or in batches, in cartons. Layers should be separated by greaseproof paper or cellophane.
Thawing and serving Thaw cold sliced poultry in its wrappings in the refrigerator for 3 hours, then separate and put on absorbent paper to take up moisture. Heat poultry in gravy or sauce in the oven 180° C, 350° F, Gas 4 for 25 minutes. Thaw fried chicken in its wrappings for 3 hours in the refrigerator, to eat cold, or heat at 230° C, 450° F, Gas 8 for 30 minutes.
Storage time 1 month.
Special notes Whole roast birds do not freeze successfully for cold dishes; on thawing they exude moisture and become flabby.

PREPARING AND PACKING GAME

Young and well-shot game birds, hares and rabbits may be frozen in the raw state. Old or badly shot game is best cooked before freezing. Game must be cooled and hung to the required

Chicken joints with suprême sauce

state before freezing; for practical purposes it should also be plucked or skinned, and drawn if this is part of the normal preparation.

GROUSE, PHEASANT, PARTRIDGE

Preparation and packing Remove all shot, and clean the wounds. 'Bleed' as soon as shot, keep cool and hang to individual taste. Pluck, draw and truss neatly. Pad bones with grease-proof paper. Pack in polythene bags, excluding all air. If birds are old or badly shot, prepare as Cooked Game.

Thawing and serving Thaw in wrappings in the refrigerator for slow even thawing, allowing 5 hours per lb. At room temperature, allow 2 hours per lb. Start cooking as soon as the game is thawed, while it is still cold, to prevent loss of juices.

Storage time 6–8 months.

PLOVER, QUAIL, SNIPE, WOODCOCK

Preparation and packing Prepare and pack as other game but do not draw.

Thawing and serving Thaw in wrappings in the refrigerator, allowing 5 hours per lb, and start cooking as soon as thawed, while it is still cold.

Storage time 6–8 months.

PIGEONS

Preparation and packing Prepare as for other game. Since pigeons are rarely served plainly roasted, it is more practical to cook the birds for use in casseroles or pies before freezing.

Thawing and serving Thaw in wrappings in the refrigerator, allowing 5 hours per lb.

Storage time 6–8 months.

HARES AND RABBITS

Preparation and packing Behead hares and rabbits and 'bleed' as soon as possible. Hang for 24 hours in a cool place. Skin, clean and wipe with a damp cloth. Cut into joints and

Grilled pigeons

wrap each piece in cellophane, then pack joints in usable quantities in polythene bags for storage.
Thawing and serving Thaw in wrappings in refrigerator, allowing 5 hours per lb.
Storage time 6–8 months.

VENISON

Preparation and packing Having cleaned the shot wounds, keep carcass in good condition, and as cold as possible until butchering is possible. Behead and bleed the animal, skin and clean, wash and wipe it. Hang in a very cool place for 5–6 days. Cut in joints and pack in freezer paper, foil or polythene bags. It is best to use only the best joints for freezing and to treat the rest as mince, casseroles or pies.
Thawing and serving Thaw in wrappings in refrigerator for 4 hours, then remove the wrappings, pour the marinade over (see special notes) and continue thawing, allowing 5 hours per lb. Use strips of fat bacon for roasting.
Storage time 8–10 months.
Special notes Venison will be less dry if marinaded during thawing. Make the marinade from $\frac{1}{2}$ pint red wine, $\frac{1}{2}$ pint vinegar, 1 large sliced onion, parsley, thyme and bayleaf. Turn meat frequently while thawing and marinading. Use the marinade in casseroles.

Fish and Shellfish

Fish should be no more than 24 hours old when frozen, and shop-bought fish is rarely suitable except for the smoked varieties. Fish should only be stored for the minimum time in the freezer. White fish (cod, plaice, sole, whiting) will keep for a maximum of 6 months; fatty fish (haddock, halibut, herring, mackerel, salmon, trout, turbot) will store for 4 months; shellfish for no longer than 1 month. But smoked fish will keep up to 12 months.

Cooked fish is hardly worth freezing, since reheating will spoil its flavour and rob the fish of nutritive value, and fish should never be overcooked. Dishes such as Fish Cakes* are, however, useful for quick meals.

CLEANING THE FISH

Fish for freezing should be scaled if necessary, and the fins removed. Small fish can be left whole. Large fish may be left whole without heads or tails, or can be divided into steaks.

Flat fish and herrings are best gutted, and flat fish are easier to cook later if skinned and filleted. Fatty fish should be washed in fresh water, but other fish should be washed in salt water, removing all blood and membranes.

DRY PACK

This is the most commonly used pack for fish. They should be separated by a double thickness of cellophane, then wrapped in freezer paper, foil or polythene, or put into cartons. The wrappings must be close to the fish to exclude air which will dry the fish and remove its flavour. Freeze quickly in coldest part of freezer.

BRINE PACK

Fish prepared by this method should not be stored longer than 3 months; it is not suitable for fatty fish. Dip the fish into cold salted water (1 tablespoon salt to 1 quart water), drain and wrap in freezer paper, foil, polythene or cartons. Freeze quickly after packing.

ACID PACK

The colour and flavour of fish is preserved by citric acid, and the development of rancidity is retarded by ascorbic acid. Fish can be dipped in a solution of 1 part ascorbic-citric acid powder to 100 parts water before draining and wrapping. This powder can be made up by a chemist.

SOLID ICE PACK

This method saves wrapping material, but the packs may take up more freezer space. Fish should be separated by double paper, then packed into refrigerator trays or loaf tins, covered with water, and frozen into solid blocks. This can be used for a quantity of small fish, steaks or fillets. The fish can also be frozen in water in large waxed tubs, covering the fish to within $\frac{1}{2}$ inch of the top and crumbling a piece of cellophane on top of the fish before putting on lid.

GLAZING WHOLE FISH

Large whole fish such as salmon, salmon trout, haddock or halibut can be glazed. The fish should be cleaned, then put against the freezer wall in the coldest part of the freezer without wrappings. When the fish is frozen solid, it should be dipped very quickly in cold water to form a thin coating of ice. After returning the fish to the freezer for 1 hour, repeat the process, continuing until ice is $\frac{1}{4}$ inch thick. The fish can be stored without wrappings for 2 weeks, or can be wrapped in freezer paper or foil for longer storage.

THAWING AND COOKING

Fish should be thawed slowly in unopened wrappings, preferably in the refrigerator. Allow 6 hours in a refrigerator or 3 hours at room temperature for 1 lb of fish. Complete thawing is not necessary, except for frying, and frozen fish can be used for all types of recipes.

WHITE FISH
(Cod, Plaice, Sole, Whiting)

Preparation and packing Clean fish and prepare in dry pack, brine pack, acid pack or solid pack.
Thawing and serving Thaw in wrappings in refrigerator for 6 hours, or at room temperature for 3 hours.
Storage time 6 months.

FATTY FISH
(Haddock, Halibut, Mackerel, Salmon, Trout, Turbot)

Preparation and packing Clean fish and prepare in dry

Wrap fish in foil before freezing—and after thawing and grilling

Dressed lobster

pack, acid pack or solid pack.
Thawing and serving Thaw in wrappings in refrigerator for 6 hours, or at room temperature for 3 hours.
Storage time 4 months.
Special notes Avoid salt in cleaning or packing fatty fish as this will cause rancidity during the freezing process.

SMOKED FISH
(Bloaters, Kippers, Haddock, Trout)

Preparation and packing No special preparation is necessary, but these fish should be wrapped in foil, freezer paper or polythene, and overwrapped.
Thawing and serving Thaw, still wrapped, in the refrigerator for 3 hours.
Storage time 12 months.

CRAB

Preparation and cooking Crab should be freshly caught and frozen immediately after cooking. Cook, drain and cool thoroughly. Clean and remove all edible meat. Pack into bags or small cartons, leaving $\frac{1}{2}$ inch headspace.
Thawing and serving Thaw in container, in the refrigerator, and serve very cold.
Storage time 1 month.

LOBSTER AND CRAYFISH

Preparation and packing Cook fish, cool and split. Take flesh from shell, and pack it into bags or cartons, leaving $\frac{1}{2}$ inch headspace.
Thawing and serving Thaw in container, in the refrigerator, and serve very cold.
Storage time 1 month.

OYSTERS AND SCALLOPS

Preparation and packing Wash in salt water and open carefully.
Scallops Wash in salt water, allowing 1 teaspoon salt to 1 pint water. Pack into cartons, covering with water and allowing $\frac{1}{2}$ inch headspace.
Oysters Save the liquid when opening oysters. Wash in salt water and pack as for scallops, covering with the liquid.
Thawing and serving Thaw in container, in the refrigerator. Use scallops for cooking; oysters may be eaten raw or cooked.
Storage time 1 month.

SHRIMPS AND PRAWNS

Preparation and packing Cook and cool in the cooking water. They may be frozen in their shells with heads removed, but this involves later preparation. It is best to remove shells, pack tightly in bags or cartons, leaving $\frac{1}{2}$ inch headspace, and seal. Shrimps may be packed in waxed cartons and covered with melted spiced butter.

Thawing and serving Thaw in wrappings in refrigerator. Serve cold or use in cooked dishes.

Storage time 1 month.

Stocks, Soups, Sauces and Garnishes

The advance preparation and freezing of stocks, soups and sauces is a valuable aid to kitchen economy; vegetables can be preserved in a useful form when they are cheap, stock can be kept safely, and much time can be saved in the final preparation of cheap meals.

STOCKS AND SOUPS

All stock and soup for freezing should be cooled quickly, and all surplus fat should be removed as this separates during storage. Pack in watertight containers allowing $\frac{1}{2}$ inch headspace for wide-topped containers and $\frac{3}{4}$ inch headspace for narrow-topped containers.

Soup may also be stored in blocks if freezer space is limited. These blocks should be prepared by freezing the liquid in loaf tins or freezer boxes lined with foil, the solid blocks being wrapped in foil for storage.

SAUCES

Sweet and savoury sauces may be frozen, either in a basic form such as white sauce to be used later with other ingredients, or in complete form ready for immediate use. Mayonnaise and custard sauces do not freeze well; the ingredients freeze at different rates and give unsatisfactory results.

Sauces may be stored in ice-cube form, or in 'bricks', using the same method as for stock and soups.

STOCK AND BOUILLON

Preparation and packing Prepare stock or bouillon from meat, poultry, bones and/or vegetables. Strain, cool and remove fat. To save freezer space, concentrate until liquid is reduced by half. Pack in brick or ice-cube form, or in containers

Basic white and brown sauces on meat dishes. Bot are garnished with mushrooms and puff pastr flavours, but the brown dish has fried bread triangle and chopped parsley too

leaving 1 inch headspace.
Thawing and serving Heat gently over direct heat and use as required.
Storage time 1 month.

THICK SOUPS

Preparation and packing Prepare soup to basic recipes, but use cornflour if a thickening agent is required. Porridge oats may be used for meat soups. But rice flour gives a glutinous result. Do *not* add rice, pasta, barley or potatoes. Milk and cream are better added when soup is reheated.

Pack in brick form, or in containers, leaving 1 inch headspace.
Thawing and serving Heat in a double boiler if curdling is likely to occur, otherwise over direct heat, stirring well for smoothness.
Storage time 2 months.
Special notes Soup tends to thicken during storage. It is better to season after thawing.

BASIC SAUCES
(White and Brown)

Preparation and packing Basic sauces such as White Sauce* and Brown Sauce* can be frozen in their simplest form, to be

A rich tomato sauce with wine added before freezing

finished when thawed, or may have flavouring additions made before freezing. Cornflour should be used instead of flour when thickening is required to avoid curdling on reheating. Sauces of this type are best packed into waxed or rigid plastic containers in $\frac{1}{2}$-pint and 1-pint quantities.
Thawing and serving Reheat in a double boiler, stirring well for smoothness, and make required additions.
Storage time 1 month.

OTHER SAUCES AND GRAVY

Preparation and packing These may be added to pies or casseroles, or poured over cold meat or poultry slices. Only those thickened with cornflour are suitable for freezing. Small quantities may be frozen by the ice-cube method, wrapping individual cubes in foil for storage.
Thawing and serving Follow the directions for thawing pies, casseroles or meat in sauce. Frozen cubes may be added to soups or casseroles, or heated in a double boiler to serve with meat or fish.
Storage time 1 month.

ROUX

Preparation and packing Make a quantity of roux allowing 1 lb butter to 8 oz plain flour. Freeze tablespoons on baking sheets and pack in waxed or rigid plastic container for storage.
Thawing and serving Add frozen spoons of roux to hot liquid, stirring well and cooking gently to the required thickness.
Storage time 4 months.

FRUIT SAUCES

Preparation and packing Fruit sauces can be made from sieved fresh fruit, or fruit stewed in a little water, sieved and sweetened to taste. Sauces can also be made from fruit juice, sweetened and thickened with cornflour. These should be packed into small containers or ice-cube trays, the cubes being wrapped in foil for storage.
Thawing and serving Thaw in the container in the refrigerator for 2 hours, to serve cold. Alternatively, heat in double boiler, stirring gently.
Storage time 12 months.

MEAT SAUCE

Preparation and packing Sauces for serving with pasta, such as Spaghetti Sauce containing meat, freeze very well.

After cooking, cool thoroughly, pack into containers in usable quantities.
Thawing and serving Heat gently in a double boiler, adjusting seasonings.
Storage time 1 month.

TOMATO SAUCE AND PURÉE

Preparation and packing Tomato Sauce* and concentrated purée are best frozen in small waxed or rigid plastic containers, or in ice-cube trays, each cube being wrapped in foil for storage.
Thawing and serving Heat gently in a double boiler, stirring well. Small cubes of sauce or purée can be put into soups or stews while still frozen and gently stirred to blend into other ingredients.
Storage time 12 months.

GARNISHES

Preparation and packing Sprigs of herbs such as parsley and mint may be frozen in small foil packages or polythene bags. Strawberries with hulls and cherries on stalks can be fast frozen on trays, then packed in polythene bags.
Thawing and serving Put herbs on serving dishes and serve at once as they become limp on thawing. Put strawberries or cherries straight on to puddings or into drinks.
Storage time 12 months.

SOUP GARNISHES

Preparation and packing Use herbs and flavoured butters. Also lightly toast cubes of bread and pack in polythene bags to serve as croûtons. Make croûtons about $\frac{1}{2}$ inch thick.
Thawing and serving Put cubes of herbs or flavoured butters into hot soup just before serving. Thaw croûtons in wrappings at room temperature, or put directly into hot soup.
Storage time 1 month for croûtons.

BUTTER BALLS

Preparation and packing Make butter balls, curls or shapes and place on baking sheet. Freeze, then pack in polythene bag for storage.
Thawing and serving Put on serving dishes and leave at room temperature for 1 hour.
Storage time 6 months unsalted butter; 3 months salted butter.

FLAVOURED BUTTERS

Preparation and packing Cream butter and flavour with herbs, essences and seasoning, according to end use. Pack in small containers or in ice-cube trays, wrapping each cube in foil after freezing for easy storage. Butter may also be formed into a cylinder and wrapped in greaseproof paper, then in polythene.

Thawing and serving Thaw at room temperature for 2 hours before using for spreading. Cut slices from cylinders of flavoured butter to put on hot meat or fish.

Storage time 6 months unsalted butter; 4 months salted butter.

Special notes Parsley, garlic or shrimp are useful flavourings.

Dairy Produce

Dairy produce needs great care in preparation and packing for the freezer, but results can be good, and useful savings can be effected if bulk supplies are obtainable.

BUTTER AND MARGARINE

Preparation and packing Freeze in original wrappings, with packages overwrapped in polythene bags for easy storage.

Freeze only really rich, thick cream like this

A hot cheese soufflé made with frozen cheese and eggs

Thawing and serving Only thaw enough fat at a time for one week's use.
Storage time Unsalted fats 6 months; salted fats 3 months.

MILK
Preparation and packing Pack in cartons, allowing 1 inch headspace. Only freeze in small quantities which can be used quickly at one time. Milk should be pasteurized and homogenized.
Thawing and serving Thaw in cartons at room temperature.
Storage time 1 month.
Special notes Emergency supplies are rarely necessary in the freezer, with today's dried products and 'long life' milk available, but a surplus *can* be stored in this way.

CREAM
Preparation and packing Cream for processing should be pasteurized and cooled rapidly, and packed in waxed containers leaving 1 inch headspace. 1 tablespoon sugar to each pint of cream will improve the keeping time. Cream must contain 40% butterfat; low butterfat cream tends to separate.
Thawing and serving Thaw in container at room temperature, and beat lightly with a fork to restore smoothness. Use with puddings, or for making ice cream.
Storage time 4 months.
Special notes The texture of frozen cream can be heavy and grainy, but light beating will improve it. If used in hot coffee, the oil will rise to the surface. Only really good, thick cream responds well to freezing.

CHEESE

Preparation and packing Hard types of cheese such as Cheddar freeze most satisfactorily. Freeze in small quantities sufficient for one or two days' supply (i.e. 8 oz or less). Divide large cheeses and repack in small quantities. Divide slices with double cellophane, and wrap in foil or freezer paper.
Thawing and serving Thaw in wrappings at room temperature, allowing $1\frac{1}{2}$ to 2 hours. Cheeses are best cut when still slightly frozen as they are less likely to crumble.
Storage time 6 months.
Special notes Camembert, Port Salut, Stilton, Danish Blue and Roquefort may be frozen successfully, but tend to crumble. All cheeses must be carefully wrapped and sealed to avoid drying-out and cross-contamination.
Alternative methods

1 Grate cheese, and pack it in small quantities in containers or polythene bags. The cheese may be mixed with breadcrumbs before freezing.
2 Mix cheese with white sauce and freeze in small containers, or add sauce to leftover vegetables or poultry for freezing in containers or in the form of pies or flans.

Thawing and serving Sprinkle frozen grated cheese, or cheese and crumbs, on meat or fish dishes or vegetables, or thaw for 1 hour in its container in the refrigerator and add to stuffings or sauces.
Storage time 1 month.

CREAM AND COTTAGE CHEESE

Preparation and packing Cream cheese tends to separate on thawing. It is best blended with heavy cream to be used as a cocktail dip. Pack in waxed tubs or rigid plastic containers.
Cottage cheese should be packed in waxed tubs or rigid plastic containers, and must be frozen quickly to avoid water separation on thawing.
Thawing and serving Thaw in containers in refrigerator, preferably overnight. Blend cream cheese with a fork to restore its smoothness.
Storage time 4 months.

EGGS

Preparation and packing Eggs must be very fresh and of top quality. They should be washed and broken into a dish before processing to be checked for quality. Pack in small or large containers according to end use. Pack in waxed or rigid plastic

containers, or in special waxed cups for individual eggs. Eggs can be frozen in ice-cube trays, each cube being wrapped in foil, then bagged in polythene for storage. Eggs can be frozen whole, or the yolks and whites can be frozen separately. Salt or sugar prevents too much thickening.
Yolks Mix lightly with a fork. Mix with ½ teaspoon salt to 6 yolks, or ½ tablespoon sugar to 6 yolks. Label carefully.
Whites No pre-freezing treatment necessary.
Whole eggs Blend lightly with a fork but avoid getting in much air. Add ½ teaspoon salt or ½ tablespoon sugar to 5 eggs. Label carefully.
Thawing and serving Thaw in the unopened container in the refrigerator. For rapid use, thaw unopened at room temperature for 1½ hours. Use as fresh eggs, but use up quickly as quality deteriorates when they are left to stand. Egg whites may be kept for 24 hours in a refrigerator after thawing.
Storage time 8–10 months.
Special notes Eggs should not be frozen in their shells, as the shells may crack and the yolks harden and will not beat smoothly into the whites. When eggs are packed in quantity, their equivalent in liquid measure for use in cooking is:

2½ tablespoons whole egg = 1 egg
1½ tablespoons egg white = 1 egg white
1 tablespoon egg yolk = 1 yolk

Desserts and Ices

Nearly all sweet courses, and all ices, can be stored in the freezer. Additionally, such items as pancakes and sponge-cakes, which have been stored, can be quickly transformed with fruit, cream, ice cream or sweet sauces to make a superb finish to a meal. Only milk puddings are not successful in the freezer, becoming mushy or curdled on thawing.

ICE CREAM PREPARATION

Ices for the freezer are best made with pure cream and gelatine or egg yolks. Evaporated milk can be used if the unopened tin is boiled for ten minutes, cooled and chilled overnight in the refrigerator, but the flavour is not as good.

A crank attachment in the freezer will give very smooth ice cream; but it is expensive, and, instead, ice cream can be well beaten with a mixer or liquidizer during freezing. Egg, gelatine, cream or sugar syrup will stop ice crystals forming, and gelatine gives a particularly smooth ice. Whipped egg whites give lightness. Too much sugar prevents freezing, but freezing diminishes sweetness; a correct proportion is one part sugar to four parts liquid. Flavourings should be strong and pure.

Ice cream ready to be frozen should be packed into trays and chilled until just solid about $\frac{1}{2}$ inch from the edge. The mixture should then be beaten and frozen again, and beaten every hour for smoothness until packed for storage. It is often convenient to make ice cream in the ice-making part of the refrigerator where it can be given constant attention, and to pack and transfer it to the freezer for storage after the final beating.

ICE CREAM

Preparation and packing Make Cream Ice*, Custard Ice* or Gelatine Ice*, flavouring to taste, and pack in containers of rigid plastic, or in waxed containers.
Thawing and serving Serve straight from freezer.
Storage time 12 months.

FRESH FRUIT ICES

Preparation and packing Ices made from fresh fruit purée and cream freeze well. Prepare Fresh Fruit Ice* and add some pieces of fruit if liked. Pack in waxed or rigid plastic containers.
Thawing and serving Serve straight from freezer.
Storage time 12 months.
Special notes Raspberries, strawberries and apricots are particularly good for this type of ice cream.

A party sundae: both ice cream and sauce come from the freezer

Basic cold sweet soufflé, decorated after thawing

SORBETS

Preparation and packing Water ices prepared with fruit juice, sugar syrup and gelatine do not freeze completely hard in storage. They may be packed into waxed or rigid plastic containers. For party presentation, orange or lemon sorbet can be packed into clean fruit skins and wrapped in foil for storage.
Thawing and serving Serve straight from freezer. If the ice has been packed in containers, it may be scooped out into clean fruit skins and returned unwrapped to the freezer for 1 hour before serving, so that the skins are frosted.
Storage time 12 months.

BOMBES OR MOULDS

Preparation and packing Double-sided moulds may be bought for making moulds, but any metal mould or bowl may be used such as a jelly mould. Soften ice cream slightly before filling the mould. If packing in layers of different flavours, put

in the first layer and freeze for one hour before adding the next layer, to avoid mixing of colours and flavours. Fruit or liqueurs may be added to the ice cream, or fruit can be used to fill the centre of a mould. Wrap in foil for storage.
Thawing and serving Unmould on to chilled plate, using cloth wrung out in hot water to release ice cream. Wrap in foil and return to freezer for one hour before serving.
Storage time 12 months.

MOUSSES AND COLD SOUFFLÉS

Preparation and packing Mixtures of eggs, cream, and sometimes fruit and egg whites, freeze well, and the granular effect of gelatine does not show in these creamy sweets as it does in plain jelly. They are best prepared in the dishes in which they will be served if these will withstand the low temperature of the freezer.
Thawing and serving Thaw in refrigerator for 8 hours.
Storage time 1 month.
Special notes Chocolate and lemon flavours are particularly good.

CHEESECAKE

Preparation and packing Both baked and gelatine-set cheesecakes freeze well. They are best made in cake tins with removable bases, cooled and frozen unwrapped, then packed in foil and rigid containers to avoid damage.
Thawing and serving Thaw in refrigerator for 8 hours.
Storage time 1 month.

ICEBOX CAKES

Preparation and packing Follow the recipe for Icebox Cake, or your own, arranging biscuits and creamed mixture on a piece of cardboard covered with foil. Wrap in foil.
Thawing and serving Remove wrappings and thaw in the refrigerator for 3 hours before covering with whipped cream.
Storage time 1 month.

STEAMED AND BAKED PUDDINGS

Preparation and packing Make standard sponge pudding or cake mixture recipes, and steam or bake in foil containers. Cool and cover with foil or put into polythene bags for storage.
Thawing and serving Thaw at room temperature for 2 hours, then steam for 45 minutes.
Storage time 12 months.

Bread, Cakes, Biscuits and Pastry

All types of bread, cakes and biscuits freeze extremely well. They can be frozen unbaked or ready-to-serve. Biscuits are better cooked after freezing.

UNCOOKED YEAST MIXTURES

Unbaked yeast mixtures can be frozen for up to 2 weeks, but proving after freezing takes a long time, and the texture may be heavy. Unbaked dough must be proved once before being frozen in bulk, or, better still, shaped ready for baking. Surfaces should be brushed with oil or unsalted melted butter to prevent a tough crust forming. Dough must be thawed in a moist warm place, and greater speed in thawing will give a lighter texture. The bread must be proved before baking.

UNCOOKED CAKE MIXTURES

Cake batter can be frozen uncooked in cartons, or in rustless baking tins, and will keep for 2 months. But the resulting cakes will lose volume in cooking, and if they are thawed for too long will be heavy. There is little advantage in freezing uncooked cake mixtures.

INGREDIENTS

Fresh ingredients of good quality must be used for baked goods to be frozen as stale flour deteriorates quickly after freezing. Butter is preferable for good flavour, but margarine gives a light texture and can be used in strongly flavoured cakes such as chocolate. Egg yolks and white freeze at different speeds, so eggs should be whisked thoroughly to blend them before being incorporated in mixtures for freezing.

FLAVOURINGS

Highly spiced foods can develop off-flavours during freezing, so spice cakes are not recommended for freezing. Synthetic flavourings also develop off-flavours and should be avoided, e.g. use a vanilla pod or vanilla sugar instead of a synthetic essence.

ICINGS, FILLINGS AND DECORATIONS

Cakes should not be filled with cream, jam or fruit before freezing as cream will crumble and the other fillings will make the cakes soggy. Boiled icings and those made with cream or egg whites do not freeze well either; they tend to crumble on thawing. The best icings are those made with fat and sugar.

Ring doughnuts

Cakes should *not* be decorated before freezing as any moisture absorbed by the decorations during thawing will spoil the appearance of the cake. You can add them just before serving time.

PACKING AND FREEZING

Bread, buns and un-iced cakes can be frozen in polythene bags in convenient quantities. Small iced cakes are better packed in boxes to avoid being crushed. Freeze iced cakes unwrapped, then pack them in boxes or bags for storage, with greaseproof paper or cellophane separating layers. Wrappings should be removed before thawing iced cakes to allow moisture to escape and to avoid smudging.

BREAD AND BUNS

Preparation and packing Cooked yeast mixtures freeze best when 24 hours old. Pack in polythene bags in required quantities.

Thawing and serving Thaw in wrappings at room temperature; a $1\frac{1}{2}$ lb loaf will take 3 hours to thaw. Bread may be thawed in a moderate oven, but will become stale quickly.

Storage time 8–12 months.

DOUGHNUTS

Preparation and packing Pack in polythene bags. Home-made doughnuts must be well drained when removed from fat and are best frozen without being rolled in sugar.
Thawing and serving Remove from freezer and heat at once at 200° C, 400° F, Gas 6 for 8 minutes, then roll in castor sugar.
Storage time 1 month.
Special notes Jam in doughnuts may make them a little soggy in thawing, so ring doughnuts are preferable for freezing.

CROISSANTS AND BRIOCHE

Preparation and packing Pack in polythene bags and store carefully to avoid crushing and flaking. Or pack in boxes in layers with paper between.
Thawing and serving Thaw in wrappings at room temperature for 30–45 minutes and heat lightly in oven or under grill. Brioche may be heated with tops cut off and centres filled with sweet or savoury mixtures.
Storage time 2 months.

Croissants

DANISH PASTRIES

Preparation and packing Pastries may be frozen un-iced or with a light water icing. Pack in foil trays with foil, or in boxes to avoid crushing.
Thawing and serving Thaw at room temperature, removing wrappings if iced, for 1 hour. Heat lightly in oven if liked.
Storage time 2 months.

MUFFINS AND CRUMPETS

Preparation and packing Pack in usable quantities in polythene bags.
Thawing and serving Thaw in wrappings at room temperature for 30 minutes, then toast.
Storage time 10–12 months.

FRUIT AND NUT BREADS

Preparation and packing Do not overbake, and cool quickly. Pack in foil or polythene.
Thawing and serving Thaw in wrappings at room temperature for 1 hour. Slice while partly frozen to prevent crumbling, and spread with butter.
Storage time 10–12 months.

SCONES

Preparation and packing Prepare according to the Basic Scone Mixture*, adding fruit or cheese if liked. Pack in usable quantities in polythene bags.
Thawing and serving Thaw in wrappings at room temperature for 1 hour, or heat at 180° C, 350° F, Gas 4 for 10 minutes with a covering of foil.
Storage time 2 months.

PANCAKES, GRIDDLECAKES AND DROP SCONES

Preparation and packing Cool thoroughly before packing. Pack large thin pancakes with layers of cellophane or greaseproof paper like a cake, and wrap in foil or polythene. Pack griddlecakes and drop scones in boxes, foil or polythene bags.
Thawing and serving Thaw block of pancakes in wrappings at room temperature, or separate before thawing. Heat in low oven or on a plate over steam, covered with a cloth. Pancakes may be filled after thawing and before heating. Thaw griddlecakes and drop scones in wrappings at room temperature for 1 hour.
Storage time 2 months.

Special notes Pancakes may be filled and/or covered with sauce before freezing, but will then only store for 1 month.

SAVARINS AND BABAS

Preparation and packing Enriched yeast doughs incorporating eggs and sugar store well in the freezer, either with or without syrup poured over. Pack in foil or polythene, or in a box if syrup is used.
Thawing and serving Thaw at room temperature without wrappings, pouring on warm syrup if cake has been frozen without it. Additional sauce may be used even if cake has been frozen ready for eating.
Thaw 2–3 hours.
Storage time 3 months.

SPONGE-CAKES AND ICED CAKES

Preparation and packing The same treatment applies to fatless sponges and those with fat; to iced and un-iced cakes; to plain cake mixtures such as Madeira Cake; and to cakes flavoured with chocolate and coffee. Delicate cakes are best packed in boxes to avoid crushing. Other cakes can be wrapped in foil or polythene.

1 If cakes are to be filled and iced after thawing, pack in layers with greaseproof paper or cellophane between.
2 Cakes may be filled and iced with butter icing, frozen unwrapped, then packed for storage.

Thawing and serving Thaw at room temperature, removing wrappings if cake is iced.
Storage time 10 months for fatless cakes; 4 months for cakes with fat. Unbaked cake batter stores for 2 months.

ICE CREAM CAKES

Preparation and packing Cut sponge-cake in thin layers and put together with ice cream. Pack in box or wrap in foil after quick-freezing unwrapped.
Thawing and serving Unwrap and thaw at room temperature for 15 minutes.
Storage time 4 months.

FRUIT CAKES

Preparation and packing Wrap in foil or polythene.
Thawing and serving Thaw in wrappings at room temperature.
Storage time 4 months.

Special notes Rich fruit cakes store for a long time in tins, so it is unnecessary to waste freezer space on them. Dundee cakes, sultana cakes and other light fruit mixtures freeze well.

SMALL CAKES

Preparation and packing Small iced and plain cakes may be frozen. Damage is avoided if they are made in paper or foil cases. Iced cakes are best packed in boxes in layers with paper between, and should be frozen before packing. Other cakes may be packed in polythene bags. Cake to be cut in squares may be frozen in the baking tin or one made of foil, covered with foil or polythene for storage to be cut in squares when thawed.

Thawing and serving Thaw at room temperature, removing wrappings if iced.

Storage time 4 months.

ÉCLAIRS AND CREAM BUNS

Preparation and packing Choux pastry cases should be frozen unfilled and un-iced in bags or boxes to avoid crushing.

Thawing and serving Thaw in wrappings at room temperature for 2 hours before filling and icing.

Storage time 1 month.

Apple loaf

Waffles with fruit and jam

Special notes Cases may be filled with ice cream, frozen on trays, then packed in rigid containers. They should be thawed at room temperature for 10 minutes before serving.

BISCUITS
Preparation and packing Make Basic Sugar Biscuits*, flavouring as liked. Form dough into cylinder shapes about 2 inches in diameter. Wrap in foil or polythene.
Thawing and serving Thaw in wrappings in refrigerator for 45 minutes, cut in slices, and bake at 190° C, 375° F, Gas 5 for 10 minutes.
Storage time 2 months.
Special notes Biscuits frozen before baking are crisp and light. Baked biscuits freeze well but need careful packing to avoid crushing, and freezer space need not be wasted as they keep well in tins.

WAFFLES
Preparation and packing Do not overbrown. Pack in usable quantities in foil or polythene.
Thawing and serving Heat unthawed under grill or in oven.
Storage time 2 months.

Pastry and Pies

Unbaked and baked pastry may be frozen in slab form, or prepared as pies, pasties, turnovers, flans and unfilled cases. Baked pies store for a longer period, depending on the filling, but a frozen unbaked pie has a better flavour and scent, and the pastry is crisper and flakier.

TYPES OF PASTRY AND FILLINGS

All types of pastry freeze equally well, but it is important to use a standard balanced recipe, and ingredients must be fresh as stale flour develops an unpleasant flavour after freezing and thawing. Almost all fillings can be used, except those using custard which separates. Meringue toppings toughen and dry during storage.

Hot water crust pies These may be frozen baked or unbaked to eat cold, but there are risks attached. The pie can be frozen unbaked, partially thawed and then baked, but this means that the uncooked meat will have been in contact with the warm uncooked pastry in which hot water is used during the making process, and unless the pie is carefully handled while cooling, there is a danger of organisms entering the meat. A baked pie can be frozen without the usual jelly, and the stock can be heated and poured into the pie during thawing but this may also encourage organisms. On balance, pork and game pies with hot water crust should therefore be avoided as freezer products.

SLAB PASTRY

Preparation and packing Roll pastry, form into a square and wrap in greaseproof paper, then in foil or polythene. Only pack in small quantities, to facilitate thawing.

Thawing and serving Thaw at room temperature for 2 hours, and do not hasten thawing. Pastry may crumble when rolled if you do. Cook like fresh pastry, and eat when freshly baked.

Storage time 4 months.

Special notes Do not return to freezer in baked form.

PASTRY CASES

Preparation and packing Prepare flan cases, patty cases or vols-au-vent, using foil containers if possible. Freeze unbaked or baked. Freeze choux after baking. Small cases may be packed in boxes with paper between the layers.

Thawing and serving Thaw unbaked cases for 1 hour at room temperature, then bake like fresh pastry. Thaw baked cases at room temperature before filling. A hot filling can be used and the cases heated in a low oven.

Storage time 6 months.

UNBAKED PIES

Preparation and packing Prepare with or without a bottom crust, preferably in a foil case. Put in the cold filling. Do not cut air vents in top crust. Freeze unwrapped and then wrap in foil or polythene, or put in a polythene bag before freezing.
Thawing and serving Cut slits in top crust and bake unthawed like fresh pies, allowing 10 minutes longer than normal cooking time.
Storage time 4 months according to filling.
Special notes Freezing unwrapped will prevent sogginess.

BAKED PIES

Preparation and packing Prepare and bake pies according to recipe, and cool quickly. If possible prepare in foil, otherwise in rustproof and crackproof container. Wrap in foil or polythene.
Thawing and serving Thaw in wrappings at room temperature for 3 hours to serve cold. Heat double-crust pie at 190° C, 375° F, Gas 5 for 40–50 minutes according to size, and single-crust pies for 30–50 minutes, having put them in the oven while still frozen.
Storage time 6 months according to filling.

MEAT PIES

Preparation and packing Meat pies can be completely cooked before freezing. The filling can also be cooked and cooled, then topped with pastry and frozen unbaked. Prepare in foil containers if possible. Brush the bottom crust with melted butter or lard just before filling to prevent sogginess.
Thawing and serving Reheat cooked pies, or bake those with uncooked pastry at 200° C, 400° F, Gas 6 for required time according to size.
Storage time 2 months.

FRUIT PIES

Preparation and packing Fruit pies can be made with cooked or uncooked fillings. If the surface of the bottom crust is brushed with egg white, sogginess will be avoided. Pies may be baked or unbaked.
Thawing and serving Reheat cooked pies, or bake those which have been frozen without cooking at 200° C, 400° F, Gas 6 for required time according to size.
Storage time 4 months.
Special notes Apples tend to brown if stored in a pie for

Freeze pies or pasties for picnics or summer holiday meals

more than 4 weeks, even when treated with lemon juice, so it is better to combine frozen pastry and frozen apples to make a pie. Small fruit pies and turnovers which have been baked and frozen can be thawed in an ordinary lunch box.

FRUIT PIE FILLINGS

Preparation and packing Use the basic recipe for Fruit Pie Filling* and put into a sponge-cake tin or pie plate lined with foil. Freeze and wrap in foil for storage.
Thawing and serving Line a baking dish with pastry, put in the frozen fillings, cover with pastry and bake as usual, at 220° C, 425° F, Gas 7 for 45 minutes.
Storage time 6 months.
Special notes This is an economical way of storing fruit in quickly usable form. The addition of cornflour or flaked tapioca gives a firm filling which cuts well and does not leak.

SAUSAGE ROLLS

Preparation and packing Make sausage rolls with short,

flaky or puff pastry. Freeze unbaked rolls on trays, and pack in polythene bags or foil cases for storage. Pack baked rolls in foil cases or in boxes to avoid damage.
Thawing and serving Brush unbaked sausage rolls with egg and bake at 240° C, 475° F, Gas 9 for 20 minutes, then at 190° C, 375° F, Gas 5 for 10 minutes. Thaw baked sausage rolls in wrappings in refrigerator for 6 hours, to eat cold, or heat at 200° C, 400° F, Gas 6 for 25 minutes.
Storage time 1 month.

SAVOURY AND SWEET FLANS

Preparation and packing Open flans with savoury or sweet fillings are best completed and baked before freezing. They should be frozen without wrapping to avoid spoiling the surface, then wrapped in foil or polythene for storage, or packed in boxes to avoid damage.
Thawing and serving Thaw in loose wrappings at room temperature for 2 hours to serve cold, or reheat if required.
Storage time 2 months with fresh fillings; 1 month if made with leftover meat or vegetables.

Fruit flan

CHEESE PASTRIES

Preparations and packing Pastry made with cheese to use as the basis of canapés or savouries, or in the form of cheese straws, should be cut in shapes, and frozen on trays before packing into bags for storage.
Thawing and serving Bake unthawed at 200° C, 400° F, Gas 6 for 5–15 minutes according to size, until golden and crisp, and serve hot.
Storage time 4 months.

SAVOURY CHOUX PASTRIES

Preparation and packing Prepare choux pastry puffs and freeze when baked. Freeze fillings in waxed or rigid plastic containers.
Thawing and serving Put frozen puffs in oven heated to 150° C, 300° F, Gas 2 for 10 minutes. Cool, cut open and fill. Heat fillings gently in double boiler and cool before filling puffs.
Storage time 1 month.
Special notes Good fillings for freezing are creamed chopped chicken or ham, creamed mushrooms, creamed shrimps, and rich cheese sauce.

VOL-AU-VENT CASES

Preparation and packing Prepare pastry cases and freeze fillings separately as for Savoury Choux Pastries.
Thawing and serving Thaw cases at room temperature for 1 hour and bake as fresh pastry. Heat fillings in double boiler and cool before filling puffs.
Storage time 1 month.

QUICHE LORRAINE

Preparation and packing Bake Quiche Lorraine* in foil case, ready for freezing, or in flan ring. Cool quickly and wrap in foil. Pack in box to avoid damage.
Thawing and serving Thaw in refrigerator for 6 hours to serve cold. Heat at 180° C, 350° F, Gas 4 for 20 minutes to serve hot.
Storage time 2 months.

PIZZA

Preparation and packing Prepare Pizza* on flat foil plate and bake. Wrap in foil for storage.
Thawing and serving Unwrap and thaw at room tempera-

ture for 1 hour, then bake at 190° C, 375° F, Gas 5 for 25 minutes and serve very hot.
Storage time 1 month.
Special notes Anchovies may be omitted from topping as their saltiness may cause rancidity in the fatty cheese during storage, and they can be added at the reheating stage. Fresh herbs should be used rather than dried.

Cook's Treasures

Here are items which can usefully be stored in the freezer to speed up the preparation of meals.

PASTA DISHES
Preparation and packing Combination dishes of pasta and sauce may be packed into foil containers before the final baking, e.g. Macaroni Cheese. Cover container with foil for freezing.
Thawing and serving Heat at 200° C, 400° F, Gas 6 while still frozen, for 40 minutes until brown and bubbling.
Storage time 1 month.
Special notes Such dishes may be freshly cooked, or may be a combination of leftovers. Sauces should not be thickened with flour, but with cornflour or tomato purée.

TEA AND COFFEE
Preparation and packing Pour strong tea or coffee into ice-cube trays, then remove frozen cubes, wrap in foil and put in bags for storage.
Thawing and serving Add frozen cubes to iced tea, coffee or fruit punch.

ORANGE AND LEMON PEEL
Preparation and packing Grate peel, and pack in small waxed or rigid plastic containers.
Thawing and serving Thaw in containers at room temperature and use for cakes and puddings.
Storage time 2 months.

FRUIT JUICES AND SYRUPS
Preparation and packing Pour small quantities into ice-cube trays, then wrap cubes in foil and put in bags for storage.
Thawing and serving Put frozen cubes into fruit drinks or punch. Thaw syrup at room temperature for use as sauce, or to mix into puddings or ice cream.
Storage time 6 months.

Chicken vol-au-vent

Cheese and apple horr

Special notes In addition to flavoured syrups, surplus syrup from canned fruits may be frozen in cubes to use for fruit drinks and as a base for sweet sauces.

ICE CUBES

Preparation and packing Freeze extra quantities of ice cubes and pack in polythene bags for storage. Freeze large blocks of ice and wrap in foil. Use fruit squash or syrup for ice cubes, or add sprigs of mint, orange or lemon peel, or cocktail cherries to ordinary cubes.
Thawing and serving Put individual cubes into drinks; large blocks of ice do not dilute punches and cups so quickly.
Storage time 12 months.

ICING

Preparation and packing Prepare flavoured icings with butter and icing sugar and pack in waxed or rigid plastic containers.
Thawing and serving Thaw in container at room temperature for 2 hours, then use for filling and topping cakes.
Storage time 4 months.

GLACÉ FRUIT AND CANDIED PEEL

Preparation and packing Pack tightly in foil or polythene bag.
Thawing and serving Thaw in wrapping at room temperature for 3 hours before using.
Storage time 12 months.
Special notes These fruits keep very moist and fresh in the freezer.

NUTS

Preparation and packing Nuts may be frozen whole, chopped, slivered, or buttered and toasted, in small containers or foil or polythene bags.
Thawing and serving Thaw in wrapping at room temperature for 3 hours.
Storage time 12 months; 4 months only, if buttered and toasted.
Special notes Nuts keep moist and fresh in the freezer. Do not freeze salted nuts.

BREAD

Preparation and packing

1 Rub bread into crumbs and pack in polythene bags. Crumbs

may be mixed with soft butter, or with grated cheese.
2 Bread slices may be packed in containers or bags with greaseproof paper between.
3 Stale bread, cut in cubes, can be toasted, with or without melted butter, and packed in boxes or bags.

Thawing and serving Sprinkle frozen crumbs on meat, fish, cheese or vegetable dishes for browning and serving. Bread slices may be grated into crumbs while still frozen, or thawed at room temperature to be used for toast or sandwiches, or toasted while still frozen. Use toasted bread cubes as croûtons for soup.

Storage time 1 month.

CANAPÉS

Preparation and packing Use day-old bread cut in shapes. Spread with butter to edge of bread and use spreads suitable for freezing. Freeze unwrapped on baking trays and wrap in foil or polythene for storage.

Thawing and servicing Put on serving tray 1 hour before serving.

Special notes Canapés are best made with bread for freezing, not toast or fried bread. Avoid hard-cooked egg whites and mayonnaise in toppings. Aspic topping can be used and will keep toppings moist, but becomes cloudy after thawing.

BACON-WRAPPED APPETIZERS

Preparation and packing Wrap bacon round fillings, secure with cocktail sticks, and freeze quickly unwrapped on trays. Pack in polythene bags for storage.

Thawing and serving Put frozen appetizers under grill or in hot oven until bacon is crisp.

Storage time 2 weeks.

Special notes Suitable fillings are chicken livers, cocktail sausages, or prunes stuffed with cream cheese.

Complete Freezer Meals

Some freezer owners prefer to store all vegetables together, all cooked dishes together, and so on. Others find it more convenient to package complete meals in one polythene bag for easy storage, and this is useful if the cook is not available to complete the serving of a meal. As a compromise between the two systems, it may be practical to package sauces with pasta or with an appropriate dessert, or to prepare a complete dinner party menu and package it with a preparation timetable.

Experienced cooks will soon find their most convenient individual system, but the following plan outlines the sort of way in which frozen dishes and raw materials may be combined, with specimen timetables for final preparation and serving.

MENU
Lunch for school holidays
Tomato Juice
Spaghetti with Meat Balls in Gravy
Fruit Crumble
Preparation timetable
3 hours before meal:
Remove tomato juice from freezer and put in container in refrigerator.
30 minutes before meal:
Put meat balls in gravy into double boiler and heat gently.
Put fruit crumble into oven 200° C, 400° F, Gas 6.
20 minutes before meal:
Put frozen spaghetti into boiling water, bring back to boil, and leave to simmer.
Serving time
Season tomato juice. Reduce oven heat to 190° C, 375° F, Gas 5 for fruit crumble. Drain spaghetti and pour over meat balls and gravy.

MENU
Supper for family
Tomato Soup with Croûtons
Macaroni Cheese
Fresh Fruit Ice Cream
Preparation timetable
45 minutes before meal:
Put macaroni cheese in oven 200° C, 400° F, Gas 6.
15 minutes before meal:
Heat tomato soup in double boiler.
Serving time
Add frozen croûtons to soup. Remove fresh fruit ice cream from freezer.

MENU
Dinner party
Fish Pâté

Sausage rolls

Roast Chicken with Bread Sauce
Green Peas and Duchesse Potatoes
Icebox Cake

Preparation timetable

Overnight:
Put wrapped chicken and stuffing in refrigerator to thaw.
3 hours before meal:
Transfer fish pâté and icebox cake to refrigerator from freezer. Remove wrappings from icebox cake.
2 hours before meal:
Stuff chicken and prepare for roasting.
20 minutes before meal:
Put Duchesse potatoes in oven 200° C, 400° F, Gas 6.
10 minutes before meal:
Cook frozen peas. Heat bread sauce in double boiler, adding a little cream and seasoning.

Serving time

Bring fish pâté to table with toast. Serve chicken with bread sauce, peas and potatoes. Cover icebox cake with whipped cream.

MENU

Children's tea

Sardine Sandwiches
Sausage Rolls
Iced Chocolate Cake

Preparation timetable

4 hours before meal:
Unwrap cake and put on serving plate at room temperature. Leave sandwiches in wrappings at room temperature.
25 minutes before meal:
Put cooked sausage rolls in oven 200° C, 400° F, Gas 6.

Serving time

Trim crusts from sandwiches and cut in smaller pieces.

Recipes Designed for Freezer and Fridge

You do not need recipes for all the dishes shown in the pictures in this book. The methods of roasting, grilling and frying, steaming and boiling fish, meat or vegetables, do not change, for instance, when you cook for freezer or fridge storage. In this last chapter, therefore, we are just giving you a few basic sauces, pastry dishes, ices and baked goods which you can adapt to suit the fillings or flavourings you want to use; and some garnishes and made-up dishes which you may find unfamiliar and want to try.

Aeat Stock **Yield: 1 pint**

hin beef	**1 lb**
Vater	**1 quart**
Carrot	**1**
Onion	**1 small**
Bayleaf and parsley	
Peppercorns	**6**
alt	**½ teaspoon**

Beef bones may also be used for ooking the stock. Cover meat and bones vith water and simmer for 2 hours with d on. Cut carrot and onion into small ieces, fry very lightly and add to liquid, ogether with herbs and seasoning. immer for 2 hours, strain and cool. 'ake off fat and put stock into leakproof ontainers, allowing headspace. **Thawng and serving** Heat in saucepan ver low direct heat, and use as a basis for soups and stews. **Storage time** 1 month.

White Sauce **Yield: 1 pint**

Onion	**1 small**
Carrot	**1**
Bayleaf	**1**
Butter	**1 oz**
Milk	**1 pint**
Cornflour	**1 oz**
Salt and pepper	

Cut onion and bayleaf in slices and simmer with bayleaf in milk for 15 minutes. Melt butter and carefully work in cornflour, and cook for 2 minutes. Gradually add milk, stirring very well, and season to taste. Cool and put into containers.

Variations
Cheese Sauce – add 2 oz grated cheese.
Parsley Sauce – add 2 tablespoons chopped parsley.
Shrimp Sauce – add 2 oz peeled shrimps.
Onion Sauce – add 6 oz chopped onions softened in butter.

Thawing and serving Heat in double boiler, stirring well, and adjust seasonings. Add a little cream if liked. **Storage time** 1 month.

Brown Sauce — Yield: 3 pints

Dripping	**4 oz**
Onion	**1 large**
Carrot	**1 large**
Celery	**2 sticks**
Bacon	**2 oz**
Brown stock	**4 pints**
Tomato paste	**2 tablespoons**
Mushrooms	**4 oz**
Parsley, thyme and bayleaf	
Cornflour	**3 oz**

Melt dripping, and fry sliced vegetables and bacon until brown. Drain well. Add the vegetables and bacon, tomato paste, chopped mushrooms and herbs to the stock and simmer $1\frac{1}{2}$ hours. Thicken with cornflour mixed with a little water, and continue, simmering for 30 minutes. Strain and cool. Remove any fat and pack into containers. **Thawing and serving** Heat gently in double boiler, stirring well. **Storage time** 12 months.

Cumberland Sauce

Orange	**1**
Lemon	**1**
Water	**$\frac{1}{8}$ pint**
Port wine	**$\frac{1}{8}$ pint**
Vinegar	**2 tablespoons**
Redcurrant jelly	**$\frac{1}{4}$ lb**
Mixed mustard	**$\frac{1}{4}$ teaspoon**
Salt	
Cayenne pepper	
Glacé cherries	**6–8**

Grate the rind of the orange and lemon, carefully avoiding the pith. Simmer the rinds in the water for 10 minutes. Add the wine, vinegar, jelly and mustard and simmer them together until the jelly is completely melted. Add the juice of the orange and lemon, season to taste and cool. Chop the glacé cherries and add them to the sauce.

Aspic Jelly

Jellied veal stock	**1 quart**
Gelatine	**1 oz**
Bouquet garni (parsley, thyme, bayleaf)	
Celery	**2 sticks**
Egg whites and shells	
Sherry (optional)	**1 glass**
Vinegar	**$\frac{1}{4}$ pint**

Let the stock become quite cold, and remove every particle of fat. Put it into a stewpan with the gelatine, herbs, celery cut into large pieces, the egg whites previously slightly beaten and the shells previously washed and dried. Whisk over heat until nearly boiling, then add the wine and vinegar. Continue the whisking until quite boiling, then reduce the heat and simmer for about 10 minutes, strain till clear. Freeze, thaw and use like meat stock.

For Aspic Jelly set with Gelatine, use

Egg whites and shells	
Lemon	
Stock	**1 quart**
Gelatine	**2 oz**

White vinegar — **¼ pint**
Onion — **1**
Carrot — **1**
Celery — **2–3 sticks**
Bouquet garni
Peppercorns — **10–12**
Salt — **1 teaspoon**

Whisk the egg whites slightly. Wash he shells. Peel the lemon rind thinly, nd strain the juice. Strain the stock. Put all the ingredients into a pan, whisk over medium heat until boiling. Lower heat and simmer gently for about 20 minutes. Strain. Use as above.

Tomato Sauce — Yield: 1 pint

Tomatoes — **1 lb**
Butter — **1 oz**
Onion — **1 small**
Carrot — **1 small**
Ham — **1 oz**
Stock — **1 pint**
Parsley, thyme, bayleaf
Cornflour — **½ oz**
Salt and pepper

Cut up tomatoes roughly. Melt butter nd cook sliced onion and carrot until oft and golden. Add tomatoes, ham, tock and herbs and simmer for 30 minutes. Put through a sieve and thicken with cornflour mixed with a little water. Season to taste and simmer for 5 minutes, tirring well. Cool and put into small ontainers or ice-cube trays, wrapping ce cubes when frozen in foil for storage. **Thawing and serving** Heat in double boiler, stirring well, and adding additional flavourings as required. **Storage ime** 1 month.

Apple Sauce — Yield: ½ pint

Apples — **1 lb**
Sugar — **To your taste**
Lemon juice — **To your taste**

Using very little water, cook apples to a pulp. This is best done in the oven, in a casserole. The flavour will be better if the apples are left unpeeled. Sieve apples, and sweeten to taste, adding a little lemon juice. Cool and pack, leaving ½ inch headspace. **Thawing and serving** 3 hours at room temperature. **Storage time** 12 months.

Consommé Royale — Yield: 6 helpings

Consommé — **1 quart**
Royale Custard Shapes
Egg yolks — **2**
Salt and pepper
Milk or **stock** — **1 tablespoon**

To make the custard, mix the egg yolks with the seasoning and thc milk or stock. Strain it into a small greased basin. Stand the basin in hot water and steam the custard until it is firm. Turn out the custard, cut it into thin slices, and from these cut tiny fancy shapes with a 'brilliant' cutter. Add them to the hot consommé.

Edam Puffs — Yield: 4 puffs

Flaked cooked fish — **2 oz**
Melted butter — **2 teaspoons**
Grated Edam cheese — **2 oz**
Salt and Cayenne pepper to taste
Beaten egg — **1**
Puff pastry — **8 oz**

Mix together the fish, butter, cheese, seasonings and beaten egg. Roll out the pastry and cut into 4 rounds. Put mixture on half of each circle, and fold over pastry to make semi-circles. Bake at 220° C, 425° F, Gas 7 for 15 minutes.

Scallops

Cool and pack in a polythene bag to freeze. **Thawing and serving** Thaw in refrigerator to serve cold. Heat at 180° C, 350° F, Gas 4 for 15 minutes to serve hot. **Storage time** 2 months.

Dutch Rarebit   Yield: 2 servings

Grated Gouda cheese	**6 oz**
Butter	**1 tablespoon**
Onion	**1 medium**
Tomato pulp	**$\frac{1}{4}$ pint**
Paprika	**$\frac{1}{2}$ teaspoon**

Melt the butter and cook the finely chopped onion until soft. Add tomato pulp (sieved, tinned tomatoes are excellent) and heat through, adding paprika. Add the cheese and stir until just melted. Cool and put into a rigid container for freezing. **Thawing and serving** Hea gently in a double saucepan and pou over buttered toast. **Storage time** 1 month.

Mock Crab   Yield: 4 servings

Grated Gouda cheese	**4 tablespoons**
Paprika	**1 teaspoon**
Salt	**1 teaspoon**
Made mustard	**1 dessertspoon**
Olive oil	**3 dessertspoons**
Vinegar	**2 dessertspoons**

Put cheese into a basin. Add paprika salt, mustard, oil and vinegar and work together without breaking up the cheese. Put into a rigid container to freeze. **Thawing and serving** Thaw at room temperature for 30 minutes, spread on

Edam puffs

riangles of toast, and brown lightly ınder the grill. **Storage time** 1 month.

'ish Cakes Yield: 8 fish cakes

Cooked white fish	**8 oz**
Mashed potatoes	**8 oz**
Chopped parsley	**2 teaspoons**
Butter	**1 oz**
Salt and pepper	
Egg to mix	

Flake the fish and mix with the potatoes, parsley, melted butter and easonings. Mix with egg to bind firmly. Divide mixture into 8 portions and latten into rounds. Coat with egg and breadcrumbs and fry until golden. Cool, pack in flat box or wrap in freezer paper or foil. **Thawing and serving** Heat in oven or in frying pan with a little fat without thawing. **Storage time** 1 month.

Meat Loaf Yield: 1 meat loaf

Eggs	**2**
Milk	**$\frac{1}{2}$ pint**
Soft white breadcrumbs	**6 oz**
Salt	**$1\frac{1}{2}$ teaspoons**
Pepper	**$\frac{1}{2}$ teaspoon**
Minced chuck steak	**2 lb**

Oven heat 180° C, 350° F, Gas 4

Pan Loaf tin

Beat eggs lightly, then add milk, breadcrumbs, seasonings and minced meat. Mix well. Line loaf tin with foil, leaving 6-inch overlap of foil. Pack in meat mixture. **Either** Bake in preheated oven at 180° C, 350° F, Gas 4 for 1 hour 40 minutes, cool, fold over foil to form parcel, remove from loaf tin, and freeze foil package. **Or** Do not precook, but fold over foil to form parcel, seal and freeze. **Thawing and serving** Remove foil and reheat cooked meat loaf at 200° C, 400° F, Gas 6 for 30 minutes to serve hot. Uncooked meat loaf should be cooked at 180° C, 350° F, Gas 4 for 1 hour 40 minutes. Cooked meat loaf may also be thawed in wrappings in refrigerator to eat cold. **Storage time** 1 month.

Meat Balls — Yield: 20 meat balls

Minced raw beef	**$\frac{3}{4}$ lb**
Minced raw pork	**$\frac{1}{4}$ lb**
Dry white breadcrumbs	**2 oz**
Creamy milk	**$\frac{1}{2}$ pint**
Chopped onion	**1 small**
Salt	**$1\frac{1}{2}$ teaspoons**
Pepper	**$\frac{1}{4}$ teaspoon**
Butter for frying	

Mix minced meats and soak breadcrumbs in milk. Cook onion in a little butter until golden. Mix onion with meat and breadcrumbs, and add seasonings. Shape into 1-inch balls, using 2 spoons dipped in cold water. Fry balls gently in butter until evenly brown, shaking pan to keep balls round. Drain and cool, and pack in polythene bags or in boxes with greaseproof paper between layers. **Thawing and serving** These meat balls may be eaten cold after thawing in container in refrigerator for 3 hours. They may be fried quickly in hot fat to serve, or heated gently in tomato sauce or gravy to serve with spaghetti or rice. **Storage time** 1 month.

Beef Olives — Yield: 6 servings

Stewing steak	**$1\frac{1}{2}$ lb**
Fresh white breadcrumbs	**2 oz**
Salt and pepper	**To your taste**
Egg	**1**
Plain flour	**1 oz**
Milk	**1 tablespoon**
Chopped suet	**4 level tablespoons**
Dried herbs	**A good pinch**
Grated lemon rind	**2 teaspoons**
Dripping	**2 oz**
Onions	**8 oz**
Stock	**1 pint**

Remove any excess fat from the meat and cut it into 12 even-sized pieces. For the stuffing, mix together the breadcrumbs, milk, suet, parsley, herbs, lemon rind and seasoning. Stir in the egg to bind the mixture lightly together. Divide the stuffing between the pieces of meat and roll into neat rolls. Wind a piece of cotton round the meat to keep the stuffing in place. Add a little seasoning to the flour and roll the meat in it. Heat the dripping in a heat-proof casserole or pan and fry the meat until browned all over. Lift out the meat. Fry the sliced onions until lightly browned, then return the meat to the casserole with any remaining flour. Pour over the stock and bring slowly to the boil. Put on a lid and simmer for $1\frac{1}{4}$ hours. Cool and pack in a rigid container to freeze. **Thawing and serving** Put into a casserole, cover and heat at 180° C, 350° F, Gas 4 for 45 minutes. Serve with mashed potato.

Sweet and Sour Beef Casserole — Yield: 4 helpings

Stewing steak, cut in 1-inch cubes	**$\frac{3}{4}$ lb**
Oil	**1 tablespoon**
Seasoned cornflour	**1 oz**
Honey	**2 tablespoons**
Vinegar	**2 tablespoons**
Water	**$\frac{3}{4}$ pint**
Green pepper, sliced	**$\frac{1}{2}$**
Button mushrooms, sliced	**$\frac{1}{4}$ lb**
Prunes, soaked	**4**

Green olives, stoned	**2 tablespoons**

Preheat the oven to 180° C, 350° F, Gas 4

Melt the oil in a 2½-pint freezer-to-table-ware saucepan or casserole and gently fry the beef until the cubes are browned on all sides. Stir in the honey, vinegar and water. Then add the cornflour, blended with water.

Place the pan in the preheated oven and cook for 2 hours. After 1½ hours, add the mushrooms, prunes and olives.

Cool the dish completely and skim off the fat. Cover with a lid and seal with freezer tape. **Thawing and serving** Remove the freezer tape. Return to the oven, preheated to 180° C, 350° F, Gas 4 for 45 minutes. **Storage time** 1 month.

Chicken with Suprême Sauce

Yield: 4 helpings

Chicken	**1**
Suprême sauce	**¾ pint**
White stock (approx)	**1½ pints**

Garnish

Macédoine of vegetables or **grape garnish as below.**

Truss the chicken, poach it in the stock until tender, then divide into neat joints. Arrange the joints on a hot dish, pour the sauce over, and garnish with the chopped macédoine of vegetable piled at either end of the dish.

As an alternative garnish, toss 1 chopped red pepper and 1 cooked potato (sliced) in the sauce before pouring it over the chicken. Top with black and green grapes.

Suprême Sauce

Velouté sauce	**½ pint**
Cream	**2 tablespoons – ⅛ pint**
Egg yolk	**1**
Butter	**½–1 oz**
Nutmeg to taste	
Lemon juice	
Salt and pepper	

Heat the Velouté sauce, preferably in a double boiler. Mix the egg yolk and cream, and stir into the sauce. Cook without boiling until the egg yolk thickens. Whisk in the butter, a small pat at a time. Add a pinch of nutmeg, a few drops of lemon juice, season and use the sauce at once on the cooked chicken.

Chicken Casserole

Yield: 6 servings

Chicken	**1**
Flour	**1 oz**
Salt and pepper	
Butter or **dripping**	**2 oz**
Bacon	**4–6 oz**
Shallots or **small onions**	**4–6**
Chopped mushrooms	**2 oz**
Stock	**1 pint**

Joint the chicken and dip the joints in flour and seasoning. Melt the fat in a casserole. Fry the bacon cut in strips. Add the chicken pieces, mushrooms and chopped shallots or onions. Fry until golden brown, turning when necessary. Add hot stock to cover the chicken and simmer for 1¼ hours. Cool and pack in a rigid container to freeze. **Thawing and serving** Put the chicken into a casserole, cover and heat at 180° C, 350° F, Gas 4 for 45 minutes. **Storage time** 2 months.

Salmon Quiche

Yield: 4–6 helpings

Shortcrust pastry	**6 oz**

Chicken casserole

Beef olive

Salmon, drained	**7-oz can**
Button mushrooms, sliced	**2 oz**
Eggs, beaten	**2**
Soured cream	**$\frac{1}{4}$ pint**
Milk	**$\frac{1}{4}$ pint**
Salt and black pepper	
Cheddar cheese, grated	**3 oz**
Parsley	

Roll out the pastry and use to line an $8\frac{1}{2}$-inch fluted flan ring. Place the well-drained and flaked salmon in the base and cover with the mushrooms.

Beat the eggs into the soured cream and then add the milk. Season well with salt and pepper and stir in the cheese. Pour into the flan case and cook at 220° C, 425° F, Gas 7 for 20 minutes then reduce to 180° C, 350° F, Gas 4 for a further 30–40 minutes till golden brown and firm to the touch. **Thawing and serving** Thaw in refrigerator for 6 hours to serve cold. Heat at 180° C, 350° F, Gas 4 for 20 minutes to serve hot. Garnish with parsley. **Storage time** 2 months.

Scallops with Dutch Sauce

Yield
4 helping

Scallops	**4 mediun**
Milk	**$\frac{1}{2}$ gil**
Butter	**1 o**
Cornflour	**1 o**
Potato, mashed	**As require**
Gouda cheese	**4 oz grate**
Salt and pepper	**To your tast**
Breadcrumbs	**As require**

Prepare the scallops. Throw awa the bottom shells and all parts of th scallops except the white and orange Rinse under cold water. Poach in little milk gently until tender, about 1 minutes. Brush the shells with a littl melted butter. Pipe a border of mashe potato round the edge of each shell, an place the scallops in the shells.

Use a frozen basic sauce or make cheese sauce with the butter, cornflou and almost all the grated cheese. Pou it over the scallops. Sprinkle with th emaining cheese and the breadcrumbs. 'lace under a hot grill for 5 minutes.

Make this dish, chill and then freeze : complete, or make it from frozen ıgredients.

;reamed Liver — Yield: 4 helpings

Butter	**$1\frac{1}{2}$ oz**
Onion, peeled and chopped	**1**
Calves' liver (or lambs'), sliced	**1 lb**
Seasoned flour	
Stock	**$\frac{1}{4}$ pint**
Mixed herbs	**$\frac{1}{4}$–$\frac{1}{2}$ teaspoon**
Salt and black pepper	
Lemon juice	**1 teaspoon**
Longlife cream	**$\frac{1}{4}$ pint carton**
Long grain rice	**8 oz**

Freeze this dish complete, or use rozen ingredients.

Melt the butter in the pan and sauté he onion until soft but not coloured.)ip liver in the seasoned flour, then add o the pan. Fry gently for about 5 ninutes each side.

Add stock, herbs and lemon juice and ımmer for about 5 minutes longer. **'hawing and serving** Remove cover- ıgs and heat at 180° C, 350° F, Gas 4 or about 15 minutes. Check seasonings nd stir the cream into the sauce. Reheat gently and arrange the liver on bed of cooked rice and spoon the auce over.

Glazed Beef Loaf — Yield: 4–6 helpings

Onions, chopped	**2 medium**
Garlic, chopped	**1 clove**
Dripping or **lard**	**$\frac{1}{2}$ oz**
Minced beef	**1 lb**
Breadcrumbs, fresh	**3 oz**
Worcestershire sauce	**A few drops**
Lemon juice	**1 tablespoon**
Ground nutmeg	**$\frac{1}{4}$ teaspoon**
Mixed herbs	**$\frac{3}{4}$ teaspoon**
Ground black pepper	**1 level teaspoon**
Beef consommé	**$15\frac{1}{2}$-oz can**
Orange	**1 large, peeled**
Tomato ketchup	**2 tablespoons**
Gelatine	**2 level teaspoons**

Heat oven to 190° C, 375° F, Gas 5. Fry onion and garlic in dripping until soft, and combine with the meat, bread- crumbs, Worcestershire sauce, lemon juice, spice, herbs, seasoning, tomato ketchup and half the can of consommé.

Shape the mixture into a loaf, wrap in foil and place on a baking tray. Cook for $1\frac{1}{2}$ hours; uncover the loaf, and reduce the temperature to 170° C, 325° F, Gas 3 for the last half hour. Remove from the oven and cool quickly, then place in a cold place until quite cold. Chill or freeze at this stage, if desired. **Thawing and serving** Thaw the loaf in the refrigerator for 3 hours. Place the gelatine and the remaining consommé in a bowl over a pan of hot water, and stir until the gelatine has dissolved. Leave to cool. Arrange orange segments on top of the loaf. When the consommé is nearly set, spoon it care- fully over the meat loaf and allow to set firm. Chop any remaining consommé and use as a garnish for the loaf. **Storage time** 1 month.

Galantine — Yield: 1 galantine

Chuck steak	**1 lb**
Bacon	**4 oz**
Fine white breadcrumbs	**4 oz**
Chopped parsley	**1 teaspoon**
Chopped thyme	**1 teaspoon**
Salt and pepper	
Eggs	**2**
Pans	**Loaf tin and steamer**

Mince steak and bacon and stir in breadcrumbs, herbs and seasonings, moistening with lightly beaten egg. Put into loaf tin and steam for 3 hours. Cool under weights, turn out, and wrap in freezer paper or foil. **Thawing and serving** Thaw in refrigerator overnight, and coat with brown breadcrumbs before serving. **Storage time** 1 month.

Poultry Stuffing — for one 3-lb chicken

Suet	**2 oz**
Fresh breadcrumbs	**4 oz**
Chopped parsley	**2 teaspoons**
Chopped thyme	**1 teaspoon**
Grated lemon rind	**1 teaspoon**
Salt and pepper	
Egg	**1 medium**

Grate suet and mix all ingredients, binding with beaten egg. **Either** Pack into small cartons or polythene bags, but do not stuff birds before freezing. **Or** Form mixture into small balls, deep fry, cool, drain and pack in small cartons or polythene bags. **Thawing and serving** Thaw uncooked stuffing in container in refrigerator for 2 hours before stuffing bird. Put cooked stuffing balls into roasting tin with poultry, or into casserole, 10 minutes before serving time. **Storage time** 1 month. **Special notes** Stuffing containing sausage meat should not be frozen. Basic recipe may have the addition of 2 oz bacon, but then should not be stored for longer than 2 weeks.

Fried Chicken — Yield: 6 helpings

Chicken pieces	**2 lb**
Sour cream	**¼ pint**
Lemon juice	**1 dessertspoon**
Worcester sauce	**1 teaspoon**
Salt	**1 teaspoo**
Pepper	
Paprika	
Garlic	**2 clove**
Breadcrumbs	**4 o**

Oven heat **180° C, 350° F, Gas**

Wipe chicken pieces thoroughly. Mi together cream, lemon juice and seasor ings, chopping garlic finely, and usin a pinch each of pepper and paprika Coat in breadcrumbs and arrange i greased baking dish. Bake at 180° C 350° F, Gas 4 for 45 minutes. Coo and wrap chicken pieces individually **Thawing and serving** Put froze chicken in foil wrappings in oven an bake at 200° C, 400° F, Gas 6 for 4 minutes, uncovering chicken at the en of this time, and cooking 10 minute longer. **Storage time** 1 month.

Boiled, Mashed or Creamed Potatoes — Yield: 6 helping

Potatoes, old or **new**	**2 lb even-size**
Salt	
Chopped parsley	

Scrub the potatoes. Peel or scrap thinly, if desired. Rinse and put in saucepan with enough *boiling* water t cover, and 1 teaspoon salt per quar water. Boil gently for 15–40 minute according to age and size. Test with fine skewer. When cooked, drain, stean dry for a moment over low heat, an serve hot, sprinkled with choppe parsley.

For mashed potatoes, use:

Potatoes	**2 l**
Butter or **margarine**	**1 o**
Chopped parsley	
A little milk	
Salt and pepper	
Grated nutmeg	

Prepare and cook peeled potatoes as ›r Boiled Potatoes, pass them through sieve, or through a potato masher, or ıash with a fork. Melt the fat (in one ɔrner of the pan if the potatoes have een mashed in the pan itself) and beat ı the potatoes. Add milk gradually and eat well until the mixture is thoroughly ot, and smooth. Season well and add a ttle grated nutmeg. Serve in a hot dish. prinkle with chopped parsley.

Successful mashed potato depends pon the use of a floury type of potato, ıorough drying of the potatoes after the ater has been strained off them, and ıe thorough mashing of the potatoes efore the fat and milk are added.

For creamed potatoes, add 1 table-ɔoon cream (single or double) to ıashed potatoes.

For potato balls or croquettes, ıix 1 lb mashed potatoes with 1 oz utter and 1 beaten egg. Season well ith salt and pepper. Form into small alls or rolls. Coat twice with egg and rumbs and fry in deep fat at 190° C, 75° F, Gas 5 for 4–5 minutes. Drain ell and serve at once or freeze when ɔld. If wanted for a garnish, reheat by lunging into deep hot fat.

'otato Chips .nd Potato Straws — Yield: 6 helpings

'otatoes (medium sized) — **6**
'eep fat
alt

Scrub and rinse the potatoes. Peel ıem thinly. For chips – cut into sticks bout 2 inches long and $\frac{1}{2}$ inch wide and ıick. For straws – cut into strips the size f a wooden match. Drop them into cold ater as they are cut. Rinse and drain nd dry in a clean cloth. Put them into ıe frying-basket and lower them gently into hot deep fat at 180° C, 350° F, Gas 4. (Keep the heat fairly high as the potatoes will have cooled the fat.) When the potatoes are soft but *not* brown – about 3 minutes for chips and 1 minute for straws – lift out the basket and heat the fat to 190° C, 375° F, Gas 5. Put back the basket and leave in the fat until the potatoes are crisp and golden brown – about 3 minutes for chips and 2 minutes for straws. Drain on absorbent paper, sprinkle with salt and serve immediately or freeze.

If potato chips or straws are to be served with any other fried dish, the second frying of the potatoes to brown and crisp them should be done after the other is fried. In this way the potatoes will be sent to table in their best condition.

Baked Potatoes

Large potatoes
Milk
Butter
Salt and pepper

Scrub potatoes, prick with a fork and bake at 180° C, 350° F, Gas 4 for $1\frac{1}{2}$ hours. Scoop pulp from shells, mash with, milk, butter and seasonings and return to potato shells. Pack in heavy-duty foil. **Variations** Add cheese to potato pulp; or creamed smoked fish, creamed ham or chicken, or creamed kidneys. **Thawing and serving** Re-heat at 180° C, 350° F, Gas 4 for 40 minutes. **Storage time** 3 months (1 month if fish or meat fillings).

Duchesse Potatoes — Yield: 18

Cooked potatoes	**2 lb**
Butter	**4 oz**
Eggs	**2**
Salt, pepper and nutmeg	

Sieve potatoes and beat well with butter and eggs to a piping consistency, seasoning well. Add a little hot milk if mixture is very stiff. Pipe in pyramids on to sheets lined with oiled paper, and freeze unwrapped. Pack in polythene bags for storage. **Thawing and serving** Put on baking sheets, brush with egg and bake at 200° C, 400° F, Gas 6 for 20 minutes. **Storage time** 1 month.

Pizza — Yield: one 7-inch pizza

Plain flour	**4 oz**
Yeast	**$\frac{1}{4}$ oz**
Salt and pepper	
Tomatoes	**4 medium**
Anchovy fillets	**6**
Oregano or **marjoram**	**1 teaspoon**
Cheese	**3 oz**
Olive oil	

Oven heat **220° C, 425° F, Gas 7**

Dissolve yeast in a little tepid water and put into flour, well salted. Blend well and add a little more warm water to make a stiff dough. Knead well, form into a ball, cover with a cloth, and leave in a warm place to rise for about 2 hours until double in volume. Roll out to a 7-inch disc about $\frac{1}{4}$ inch thick. Skin and chop tomatoes, and spread on dough, seasoning well with pepper and salt; arrange anchovy fillets on top, and thin slices of cheese, and sprinkle well with herbs and olive oil. Bake at 220° C, 425° F, Gas 7 for 30 minutes. Cool and wrap in foil. Mozzarella cheese should be used, but Bel Paese can be substituted, and should only be added 10 minutes before cooking finishes as it melts quickly. **Thawing and serving** Unwrap and thaw at room temperature for 1 hour, then bake at 190° C, 375° F, Gas 5 for 25 minutes and serve very hot. **Storage time** 1 month. **Special notes** Anchovies may be omitted from topping as their saltness may cause rancidity in the fatt cheese during storage; they can b added at the reheating stage. Fres herbs should be used rather than driec

Short Crust Pastry, All-purpose

Plain flour	**$\frac{1}{2}$ l**
Pinch of salt	
Butter	**2 o**
Lard	**2 o**
Cold water	

Sift the flour and salt. Rub in the fa add baking powder and, using a knif mix to a stiff dough with cold wate Use as required.

Bake in a very hot oven 230° C 450° F, Gas 8, lower later to coo filling.

For savoury tarts, a little spice or few finely chopped herbs can be addec

Quiche Lorraine — Yield one 7-inch fla

Short pastry	**4 oz when mad**
Butter	**$\frac{1}{2}$ o**
Onion	**1 smal**
Streaky bacon	**2 o**
Egg	**1 plus 1 egg yol**
Grated cheese	**2 o**
Pepper	
Creamy milk	**1 gil**

Oven heat **190° C, 375° F, Gas**

Line 7-inch flan ring or foil dish wit pastry. Soften chopped onion and baco in butter until just golden. Put int pastry case. Lightly beat together egg egg yolk, cheese, pepper and milk. A little salt may be added if bacon is nc salty. Pour into flan case. Bake a 190° C, 375° F, Gas 5 for 30 minute

Fruit stones can be frozen and stored up to six months in the freezer

:ool and wrap in foil. Pack in rigid ›ntainer to avoid damage. **Thawing nd serving** Thaw in refrigerator for hours to serve cold. Heat at 180° C, 50° F, Gas 4 for 20 minutes to serve ot. **Storage time** 2 months.

'uff Pastry, French

or Tartlets, Patties, Vol-au-Vents, etc.

utter	**1 lb**
lain flour	**1 lb**
alt	**$\frac{1}{2}$ teaspoon**
gg yolks	**2**
:old water	**$\frac{1}{3}$ pint (approx)**

Squeeze the butter in a floured cloth › remove as much moisture as possible. ut 2 oz aside and form the remainder ıto a flat cake. Keep in a cool place. ift the flour and salt and rub in the 2 oz butter. Mix to a firm dough with the egg yolks and water, and knead quickly and lightly till smooth. Roll out into an oblong about $\frac{1}{2}$ inch thick, keeping the ends square, and enfold the cake of butter in the pastry. Press lightly with the rolling pin until the butter is flattened. Roll out into a strip as thinly as possible without allowing the butter to break through, fold in 3, seal the edges using the rolling pin, and put aside in a cool place for about 15 minutes to allow the pastry to become sufficiently cool and firm. Roll and fold it twice, half turning the pastry between each rolling and again leave in a cool place for 15 minutes. After the pastry has been rolled and folded seven times it is ready for use.

TO MAKE A VOL-AU-VENT CASE

Roll out the puff pastry to about $\frac{3}{4}$ inch thickness, and with a cutter previously dipped in flour, cut into a round or oval shape as desired. Cut cleanly without dragging or twisting the pastry. Place on a baking sheet, brush over the top of the pastry with beaten egg. With a smaller, floured cutter cut an inner ring, cutting the pastry to about ½ its depth. Bake in a very hot oven 230° C, 450° F, Gas 8. When baked, remove the lid and scoop out the soft inside.

Turkey or Chicken Tartlets

Yield: 6 tartlets

Onion, finely chopped	**1**
Butter	**1 oz**
Apricot halves	**15-oz can**
Curry paste	**2 teaspoons**
Lemon juice	**2 teaspoons**
Soured cream	**¼ pt**
Cooked, chopped turkey or chicken	**10 oz**
Tabasco sauce	**½ teaspoon**
Seasoning	**To your taste**
Frozen peas	**4 oz**
Shortcrust pastry	**10 oz**
Beaten egg to glaze	

Cook the onion in butter until golden. Add the apricot halves. Simmer for 20 minutes until reduced to a thick pulp. Thin the curry paste with a little water and add to the apricots with lemon juice. Stir in the soured cream and chopped turkey pieces. Bring to the boil and simmer gently for 10 minutes. Add the Tabasco sauce, and season to taste. Remove from heat and stir in the peas. Leave covered, to cool.

Make up the pastry in the usual way. Halve the dough and roll out one half. Cut out 5-inch rounds to line large individual patty tins. Divide the cooled turkey filling equally between the tarts. Using the remaining pastry, cut out and cover the tarts, glazing with beaten egg to make the edges stick. Pinch the edges together with thumb and forefinger and decorate the tops with pastry 'leaves Glaze with beaten egg. Cook for 15–2 minutes at 220° C, 425° F, Gas 7, or unt golden brown. **Thawing and servin** Thaw in refrigerator, to serve col Heat at 180° C, 350° F, Gas 4 for 1 minutes, to serve hot. Cover wit greaseproof paper before heatin **Storage time** 2 months.

Flaky Pastry

Flour	**1 l**
Pinch of salt	
Butter or **butter and lard**	**10 o**
Cold water to mix	
Lemon juice	**½ teaspoo**

Sift the flour and salt into a basi Divide the butter into 4 equal piec and rub ¼ of it (1 piece) into the flou If butter and lard are used, blend the together well before dividing into pieces. Mix to a soft dough with co water and lemon juice, making it th same consistency as the remainin butter.

Roll out into an oblong strip an flake another ¼ piece of the butter o the ⅔ of the pastry farthest from yo Dredge lightly with flour, fold the u covered ⅓ of the pastry over, on to the f and then fold over it the fat-flaked to ⅓ of pastry. Press the edges of the pastr 'packet' together lightly with the rollin pin, to prevent butter or air bein squeezed out. Half-turn the pastry, s that the folded edges are right and le when rolling. With the rolling pin, pre ridges in the pastry to distribute the a evenly. Roll out. Allow the dough relax in a cool place for 10 minutes.

Repeat the process twice to incorpo ate the remaining two ¼ pieces of th butter.

Put flaky pastry into a very hot ove 230° C, 450° F, Gas 8 until set, the reduce to 190° C, 375° F, Gas 5 for long as required.

'O MAKE PATTY CASES

Roll out puff or flaky pastry to a thick-ess of $\frac{1}{8}$ inch and cut into rounds with 2½-inch or 3-inch cutter. Remove the entres from half of these rounds with 1¼-inch or 1½-inch cutter. Turn the astry upside down after cutting. Ioisten the plain halves and place the nged halves evenly on top. Prick the entres. Place on a baking tray and llow to stand for at least 10 minutes in cold place. Glaze the ringed halves nd the small lids and bake in a very hot ven 230° C, 450° F, Gas 8. When aked, remove and scoop out any soft ıside part. If liked the cases can be ıade as vol-au-vent cases.

'O MAKE HORN OR :ORNET CASES

Roll out pastry thinly, then cut into :rips ½ inch wide and 12–14 inches long, Ioisten strips with water and wind ›und cornet mould from the point up-'ards with moist surface on outside. inish final overlap on underside of tin nd trim neatly. Brush with milk and ake in the middle of a very hot oven 30° C, 450° F, Gas 8. Cooking time)–15 minutes.

'O MAKE HOT WATER :RUST PASTRY

or Pork, Veal and Ham or ›aised Game Pies

lain flour	**10 oz**
alt	**½ teaspoon**
ard	**3 oz**
Iilk or **water**	**¼ pint**

Sift the flour and salt into a warm ›wl, make a well in the centre, and ›ep in a warm place. Heat the lard ıd milk *or* water together gently until ›iling, then add them to the flour, mixing well with a wooden spoon, until cool enough to knead with the hands. Knead thoroughly, use as required. Leave covered for ½ hour.

Throughout the processes of mixing, kneading and moulding, the pastry must be kept warm. But if it is too warm it will be so soft and pliable that it cannot retain its shape, or support its own weight.

Bake in a hot oven 220° C, 425° F, Gas 7, reducing heat to moderate 180° C, 350° F, Gas 4 as soon as pastry is set.

TO RAISE A PIE

The pastry must be raised or moulded whilst still warm. Reserve ¼ for the lid and leave in the bowl in a warm place covered with a cloth. Roll out the remainder to about ¼ inch thickness in a round or oval shape. Gently mould the pie with the hands; if this proves too difficult mould it over an inverted, greased and floured jam jar.

Fancy Bread Rolls
Basic Dough

Plain flour	**½ lb**
Salt	**1 level teaspoon**
Margarine	**1 oz**
Fresh yeast or	**½ oz**
dried yeast	**¼ oz**
Castor sugar	**1 heaped teaspoon**
Skim milk made from milk powder	**¼ pint**

Sift the flour and salt into a large bowl. Leave to stand in a warm place for 10–15 minutes. Rub in the margarine. Cream the yeast and sugar together until liquid. Warm the milk and stir into the yeast mixture. Make a well in the centre of the flour, pour in the liquid and mix to a soft dough. Knead for 5–10 minutes on a floured surface, until the dough is smooth and glossy. Place in a greased bowl, turn over to grease the whole surface of the dough, cover with a damp cloth, and leave to rise until doubled in size. Shape as required.

Trefoils

Divide the basic dough into 8 pieces, then divide each piece into 3 bits. Form these into balls and cluster 3 together in a patty tin. Fill 8 tins, then leave in a warm place until doubled in size. It will take about 15 minutes. Brush with beaten egg yolk and skim milk to glaze, and scatter on a few poppy seeds. Bake in a fairly hot oven, at 200° C, 400° F, Gas 6 for 15–20 minutes.

Bread Knots

Divide the dough into 8 pieces and roll each into a tube shape about 10 inches long. Tie in a loose knot. Prove and glaze as above, place on a greased baking sheet, and bake like trefoils.

Baby Cottage Loaves

Divide the basic dough into 8 pieces. Cut each piece into a smaller and larger piece. Shape into rounds. Place the larger rounds on a greased baking sheet, and put the smaller ones on top. Make a dip in the centre of each with your finger. Prove and glaze like trefoils, and bake in the same way.

Ginger Twists

Knead 2 level teaspoons ground ginger into the dough (or sift in with the flour). Divide the dough into 16 pieces and roll each out 6 inches long. Twist 2 pieces together, and place on a greased baking sheet. Prove, glaze and bake like trefoils. When cooked and cool, brush over with icing made from sifted icing sugar and water.

Croissants

Plain flour	**1 lb**
Salt	**2 level teaspoons**
Lard	**1 oz**
Beaten egg	
Hard margarine	**4–6 o**

Yeast Mixture

1 oz fresh yeast blended into ½ pin (less 4 tablespoons) water or **level tablespoon dried yeas sprinkled on the same amount c water warmed to 43° C, 110° with 1 teaspoon sugar.**

Rub the 1 oz lard into the flour. Mak a dough with the yeast mixture afte letting it stand for 10 minutes. Mix th beaten egg in with the yeast mixtur Knead the dough on a lightly floure board for 10–15 minutes until smoot Roll into a strip about 20 × 8 inches an ¼ inch thick, taking care to keep th edges straight and corners square. Softe the margarine with a knife, and divid it into 3 parts. Dot one part in flakes ove two-thirds of the dough, leaving a sma border clear. Fold in 3, folding over th unflaked portion first. Turn the doug so that the fold is one the right-hand sid Seal the edges with a rolling pin. R shape into a long strip by gently pressin the dough at intervals with a rolling pi Repeat the flaking and folding proce twice more. Place the finally shape dough in a polythene bag, and let it re in the refrigerator for ½ hour. Roll ou as before, and repeat the folding proce 3 times more. Let the dough rest in th fridge for 1 hour this time.

Roll the dough into a rectangle abou 23 × 14 inches. Let it rest for 10 minute Then trim it with a knife to 21 × 1 inches and divide the strip in ha lengthways. Cut each strip into 6 tr angles 6 inches high with a 6-inch bas Make an egg wash with 1 egg, a littl water and ½ teaspoon sugar. Brush th croissants. Roll up each triangle loosel towards its point from the opposite sid ending with the tip underneath. Curv each into a crescent moon shape.

Icing a cake after thawing

Put the shaped croissants on an un-;reased baking sheet. Brush the tops vith egg wash, put the sheet into a lightly ;reased polythene bag and leave at oom temperature for about ½ hour, intil the croissants are light and puffy. Brush yet again with egg wash, and bake n the centre of a hot oven at 220° C, 25° F, Gas 7 for 20 minutes.

Apricot Pudding — **Yield: 4 helpings**

Apricots, canned	**6 halves**
Butter or **margarine**	**3 oz**
Castor sugar	**3 oz**
Eggs	**2**
Rind of ½ lemon	
Plain flour	**3 oz**
Baking powder	**¼ teaspoon**

Grease a 1½-pint basin. Drain the pricots well and cut them into small pieces.

Cream together the fat and sugar and when really soft beat in the eggs gradually. Stir in the grated lemon rind, apricots and the sifted flour and baking powder. Turn the mixture into the basin, cover and steam steadily for 1¼–1½ hours. Serve with apricot sauce.

Apricot Sauce

Apricots, fresh or **canned**	**½ lb**
Water or **syrup from can**	**¼ pint**
Brown sugar	**1–2 oz**
Lemon juice	
Maraschino (optional)	**1 teaspoon**
Arrowroot	**1 level teaspoon**

Stone the apricots and stew them till soft in the water. When soft rub them through a hair or nylon sieve. Meanwhile crack the stones, scald and skin the kernels. Add sugar, lemon juice, liqueur (if used) and kernels to the sauce. Reheat the sauce, stirring in the arrowroot blended with a little cold water. Bring to the boil and serve.

Baked Apples

Yield: 6 helpings

Apples	**6**
Brown sugar	**6 oz**
Cinnamon or cloves	**1 pinch**
Lemon juice	

Oven heat 200° C, 400° F, Gas 6

Wash large firm fruit and remove cores, leaving $\frac{1}{4}$ inch at base to hold filling. Fill with brown sugar, a trace of spice and a squeeze of lemon juice. Bake at 200° C, 400° F, Gas 6 until apples are tender. Cool. Pack into individual waxed tubs or foil dishes. Apples may be packed into large foil dish, separated by cellophane. **Thawing and serving** Thaw in a refrigerator for 3 hours to eat cold, or heat at 180° C, 350° F, Gas 4 for 25 minutes to eat hot. **Storage time** 2 months.

Fruit Pie Filling

Yield: one 7-inch pie filling

Apples	**8 oz**
Raspberries	**1 lb**
Lemon juice	**1 tablespoon**
Sugar	**8 oz**
Tapioca flakes	**2 tablespoons**
Salt	**1 pinch**

Mix ingredients thoroughly and leave to stand for 15 minutes. Line 7-inch pie plate with foil, leaving 6-inch rim. Put filling in foil, fold over and freeze. Remove foil parcel from pie plate and store in freezer. **Variations** Mix rhubarb and orange; apricot and pineapple; or use single fruits such as pitted cherries or blackberries. **Thawing and serving** Line pie plate with pastry, put in frozen filling, dot with butter, cover with pastr lid, make air vents in lid, and bake a 220° C, 425° F, Gas 7 for 45 minutes **Storage time** 6 months.

Fruit Syrup

Raspberries, currants, strawberries, elderberries, blackberries
Sugar $\frac{3}{4}$ lb to each pint of juic

Use clean ripe fruit, and pick ove well. Add $\frac{1}{4}$ pint of water to each lb c raspberries or strawberries, and $\frac{1}{2}$ pin of water to each lb of currants, elder berries or blackberries. Cook gently fo an hour, crushing fruit down gently Turn into jelly bag and leave to drai overnight. Measure juice and add $\frac{3}{4}$ l sugar to each pint of juice. Stir well unti dissolved. Pack into containers leavin $\frac{1}{2}$ inch headspace, or freeze by ice-cub or block method.

Basic Cold Sweet Soufflé

Yield 6 helping

Lemons	
Eggs, according to size	**3–**
Castor sugar	**5 o**
Gelatine	**$\frac{1}{2}$ o**
Water	**$\frac{1}{4}$ pin**
Double cream	**$\frac{1}{2}$ pin**

Decoration

Chopped pistachio nuts

Wash lemons dry, and grate rin finely. Whisk the egg yolks, sugar, rin and lemon juice over hot water unt thick and creamy, then remove bow from the hot water and continue whisk ing until cool. Soften the gelatine in th $\frac{1}{4}$ pint water, and heat to dissolve. Hal vhip the cream. Whisk the egg whites 'ery stiffly. Add the gelatine, still hot, n a thin stream, to the egg mixture, and tir in as you do it. Fold in the cream and he stiffly whipped whites. Fold the nixture very lightly until setting is mminent, when the mixture pulls against the spoon. Pour into the soufflé lish and leave to set. Remove the paper band by coaxing it away from the mix-ure with a knife dipped in hot water. Decorate the sides with chopped, blanched pistachio nuts, and the top vith whipped cream, if liked.

This is a good 'basic' soufflé recipe. t can be flavoured and decorated with almost any flavouring and garnish, such as coffee, chocolate, fruit or a liqueur, vith appropriate small sweets or nuts as lecoration.

Custard Ice — Yield: 4 helpings

Milk	**$\frac{1}{3}$ pint**
Vanilla pod	**1**
Egg yolks	**2 large**
Sugar	**2 oz**
Salt	**Small pinch**
Thick cream	**$\frac{1}{3}$ pint**

Scald milk with vanilla pod, remove pod and pour milk on to egg yolks which have been lightly beaten with sugar and alt. Cook in a double boiler until mixture coats the back of a spoon. Cool and strain. Stir in cream. Pour into freezing trays and beat twice during a total freezing time of 3 hours. Pack into containers, cover and seal.

Gelatine Ice — Yield: 4 helpings

Creamy milk	**$\frac{3}{4}$ pint**
Vanilla pod	**1**
Gelatine	**1 dessertspoon**
Sugar	**3 oz**
Salt	**1 pinch**

Heat $\frac{1}{4}$ pint milk with the vanilla pod to boiling point. Soak the gelatine in 2 tablespoons water, and heat the bowl standing in hot water until the gelatine is syrupy. Pour the warm milk on to the gelatine, stir in sugar and salt, and add the remaining milk. Remove vanilla pod. Beat twice during 3 hours' freezing time. This mixture is particularly good with added flavourings.

Cream Ice — Yield: 4 helpings

Thin cream	**1 pint**
Vanilla pod	**1**
Sugar	**3 oz**
Salt	**1 pinch**

Heat cream with vanilla pod, remove from heat, stir in sugar and salt, and cool. Take out vanilla pod and freeze mixture to a mush. Beat well in a chilled bowl, and continue freezing for a total of 2 hours. Pack into containers for storage.

Ice Cream Flavourings

Butterscotch – cook sugar in recipe with 2 tablespoons butter until well browned and add to hot milk or cream.
Caramel – melt half the sugar in a heavy saucepan over moderate heat, and add slowly to the hot milk.
Chocolate – melt 2 oz plain chocolate in 4 tablespoons hot water and add to hot milk.
Coffee – scald 2 tablespoons ground coffee with milk or cream, and strain into other ingredients.
Peppermint – colour lightly green and flavour with oil of peppermint.
Praline – add 4 oz blanched, toasted and finely chopped almonds to caramel ice.
Ginger – add 3 tablespoons ginger syrup and 2 tablespoons chopped preserved ginger.

A frozen fruit purée can easily be made into a fruit ice for a delicious parfait

Maple – use maple syrup in place c sugar and add 4 oz chopped walnuts.

Pistachio – colour lightly green an add 1 teaspoon almond essence and 2 o chopped pistachio nuts.

Mixed flavours

(a) chocolate or butterscotch sauc swirled through vanilla ice befor packing.

(b) chopped toasted nuts or crushe nut toffee added to vanilla, coffe or chocolate ice.

(c) a pinch of coffee powder added t chocolate ice, or chocolate powde added to coffee ice.

(d) crushed strawberries, raspberries o canned mandarin oranges added t vanilla ice.

Fruit Ice

Sugar	**$\frac{1}{4}$ l**
Water	**$\frac{3}{8}$ pint (15 tablespoons**
Egg	
Baby's strained pears	**2 × $4\frac{1}{2}$-oz can**
Lemon juice	**1 lemo**
Double cream	**$\frac{1}{8}$ pin**

Boil the water and sugar for 1 minutes.

Separate the egg yolk from the whit and add the yolk to the strained pear Add the hot sugar syrup, stirring con tinuously. Stir in the lemon juice an place in a shallow container in th freezing compartment of the refrigerato When set to a creamy consistency, fol in the stiffly beaten egg white and th lightly whipped cream. Return to th freezer until stiff.

This Basic Recipe Can be Used in Several Ways:

1 Set the fruit ice in a ring mould, tur out and fill the centre with fruit.

2 Set the fruit ice in a deep container, spoon into sundae glasses and serve with pears, chocolate sauce and chopped nuts.
3 Set the fruit ice in a deep container, spoon out into an orange skin basket, and intersperse the fruit ice with the orange segments.

Fresh Fruit Ice

Yield: 4 helpings

Cream	**$\frac{3}{4}$ pint**
Fruit purée	**$\frac{1}{2}$ pint**
Castor sugar	**$1\frac{1}{2}$ tablespoons**

Whip cream lightly until just thick. Fold in fruit purée and sugar, and pour into freezer tray without stirring during freezing time. Scoop into containers for storage. Fresh raspberries, strawberries, or apricots poached in syrup are very good for this ice cream.

Sorbet

Yield: 4 helpings

Gelatine	**2 teaspoons**
Water	**$\frac{1}{2}$ pint**
Sugar	**6 oz**
Grated lemon rind	**1 teaspoon**
Grated orange rind	**1 teaspoon**
Orange juice	**$\frac{1}{2}$ pint**
Lemon juice	**4 tablespoons**
Egg whites	**2**

For lemon sorbet (variation), use all lemon juice and rind instead of the mixture of orange and lemon which gives a good orange flavour. Soak gelatine in a little of the water. Boil remaining water and sugar for 10 minutes to a syrup. Stir gelatine into syrup and cool, then add rinds and juices. Beat egg whites stiff but not dry and fold into mixture. Freeze to a mush and beat. Continue freezing, allowing 3 hours' freezing time, but do not beat. This ice will not freeze hard. Pack into containers or fruit skins.

Orange and Ginger Milk Shake

Two bought family sweet vanilla ice cream packs	
Milk	**$\frac{3}{4}$ pint**
Orange rind and juice	**2**
Stem ginger	**6 pieces**
Sugar	**$\frac{1}{2}$ oz**
Julienne strips of orange peel	

Soften $1\frac{1}{2}$ packs of the sweets of ice cream and blend together with the milk, orange rind and juice, ginger and sugar until smooth. Pour into chilled glasses. Decorate with the remainder of the ice cream cut into wedges and garnish with orange strips.

Icebox Cake

Yield: 1 large cake

Icing sugar	**6 oz**
Butter	**4 oz**

Icebox cake

Eggs — **2 medium**
Grated lemon peel — **2 teaspoons**
Lemon juice — **2 tablespoons**
Sponge finger biscuits — **48**

Cream butter and sugar until light and fluffy, and work in eggs one at a time. Gradually add lemon peel and juice and beat hard until fluffy and smooth. Cover a piece of cardboard with foil and on it place 12 biscuits, curved side down. Spread on one-third of creamed mixture. Put another layer of biscuits in opposite direction, and more creamed mixture. Repeat layers and end with a layer of biscuits. Wrap in foil. **Variation** Substitute 2 tablespoons cocoa and 1 teaspoon coffee essence for lemon juice and peel. **Thawing and serving** Remove wrappings and thaw in refrigerator for 3 hours before covering with whipped cream. **Storage time** 1 month.

Iced Coffee Cake

Butter — **7 oz**
Castor sugar — **4 oz**
Eggs — **2 large**
Coffee essence — **1 tablespoon**
Brandy — **3 tablespoons**
Victoria sandwich cakes — **2 7-inch**
Double cream — **5 oz carton**
Instant coffee powder — **1 level dessertspoon**
Icing sugar — **6 oz**
Walnuts, finely chopped — **2 oz**

Cream 4 oz butter until it is soft but not oily. Beat in the castor sugar until the mixture is fluffy and light in colour. Add the eggs one at a time, beating well after each addition. Stir in the coffee essence and the brandy. Slice each sponge into 3 layers, making 6 in all. Put one layer at the bottom of a 7-inch cake tin with a fixed base. Spoon on a fifth of the coffee cream mixture. Continue adding layers of cake and cream ending with a cake layer. Put the base of a 7-inch sandwich tin on the cake layer and weight it so that the cake and cream layers are pressed. Leave for 4 hours in the fridge, or deep freeze. **Thawing and serving** Turn out by dipping a knife in hot water and running it round the inside of the cake tin. Turn on to a serving plate. Cut the cake into 6 large wedges; push them together on a serving plate. Beat rest of butter until creamy. Gradually add the sifted icing sugar. Add the coffee powder. Spread round the sides of the cake and press the walnuts round the edge. Whip the cream; put in a piping bag and pipe a large swirl on each wedge. Decorate with coffee bean sweets.

You can complete the cake except for the whipped cream and sweets, and freeze it. **Storage time** 2 months.

Festive Gâteau

Yield 1 cake to serve 8

Plain flour — **2 oz**
Eggs — **4 large**
Castor sugar — **4 oz**
Ground hazelnuts — **1 oz**
Grated Bournville chocolate — **1 oz**
Butter, melted — **1 oz**

Filling and Decoration

Hazelnuts — **9**
Bournville chocolate — **2 oz**
Double cream — **$\frac{1}{4}$ pint**
Icing sugar sifted — **1 level tablespoon**
Grated chocolate
Fondant sweets

Pans — **2 × 7-inch sandwich tins**

Grease and line the sandwich tins; grease the paper lining also. Sift the flour twice. Whisk the eggs and sugar ogether until they are pale in colour nd thick in texture. Gently stir in the azelnuts, chocolate and flour, ensuring hat there are no pockets of flour left in he mixture. Fold in the melted butter; ivide the mixture evenly between the ins and bake in a moderate oven, 80° C, 350° F, Gas 4 for 20 minutes. 'lace a folded tea-towel on a wire tray, urn the cakes on to this to avoid marking he surface. Remove paper when cold. 'reeze. **Thawing and serving** Thaw he cake at room temperature for 1 hour. 'o complete the cake, roast the hazel-uts in a hot oven for 2–3 minutes, then emove skins by rubbing in a cloth. reak the chocolate and put into a basin anding over a pan of hot water until ielted. Leave to cool. Whip the cream; old in the icing sugar alternately with he cooled chocolate and sandwich the akes together with half the chocolate ream, then spread the remainder over he top and sides. Cover with the grated hocolate. Decorate with the sweets. **torage time** 1 month.

Iocha Nut Fudge

ournville chocolate	**4 oz**
utter	**2 oz**
nstant coffee powder	**2 level teaspoons**
ouble cream or **evaporated milk**	**4 tablespoons**
hopped walnut halves	**1 oz**
cing sugar, sifted	**1 lb**

'an **6-inch square shallow cake tin lightly oiled**

Break up the chocolate and put it vith the butter into a basin standing ver hot water. Leave to melt, then emove from heat. Stir in the coffee owder, cream or evaporated milk and uts. Gradually work in the icing sugar nd, when it is smooth, press into the tin. Leave overnight to set. Cut into 1-inch squares. Pack into polythene bags, and freeze. **Thawing and serving** Allow to stand at room temperature for 2 hours, then wrap in cellophane. **Storage time** 3 months.

Swiss Circles

Yield: about 14 biscuits

Butter	**6 oz**
Icing sugar, sifted	**1 oz**
Plain flour	**4½ oz**
Cornflour	**1½ oz**
Drinking chocolate	**1 oz**
Baking powder	**¾ level teaspoon**
Vanilla essence	**½ teaspoon**

Cream the butter and icing sugar together until light in colour and texture. Sieve the dry ingredients and gradually stir them into the creamed mixture. Add the vanilla essence. Put the mixture into a piping bag, to which is attached a star pipe and press small circles of the mixture on to greased baking trays, finishing with a star at the join. Bake in a hot oven, 220° C, 425° F, Gas 7 for 6 minutes, then lower the heat to 180° C, 350° F, Gas 4 for a further 6 minutes, until the biscuits are cooked. Leave to cool. **Thawing and serving** Thaw in wrappings at room temperature for 1 hour. Sprinkle with sifted icing sugar. **Storage time** 2 months.

Basic Sugar Biscuits

Yield: 30–40 biscuits

Butter	**4 oz**
Castor sugar	**8 oz**
Egg	**1 (or 2 egg yolks)**
Milk	**1 tablespoon**
Vanilla essence	**½ teaspoon**
Plain flour	**6 oz**
Baking powder	**½ level teaspoon**

Salt	**½ level teaspoon**

Oven heat	**190° C, 375° F, Gas 5**

Cream butter and sugar and work in egg, milk and vanilla essence. Add sifted flour, baking powder and salt and mix to a firm dough. Chill, then form into a cylinder shape about 2 inches diameter. Wrap in foil or polythene. **Variations** *Butterscotch* – 1 oz chopped nuts and brown sugar instead of castor. *Chocolate* – Add 1 oz cocoa. *Date* – Add 2 oz chopped dates. *Ginger* – Add 1 teaspoon ground ginger. *Lemon* – Add ½ teaspoon lemon essence instead of vanilla. *Orange* – Add grated rind of ½ orange and substitute orange juice for milk. **Thawing and serving** Thaw in wrappings in refrigerator for 45 minutes, cut in slices and bake at 190° C, 375° F, Gas 5 for 10 minutes. **Storage time** 2 months.

Basic Scones **Yield: 24 scones**

Plain white flour	**1 lb**
Bicarbonate of soda	**1 teaspoon**
Cream of tartar	**2 teaspoons**
Butter	**3 oz**
Milk	**¼ pint**

Oven heat	**230° C, 450° F, Gas 8**
Pan	**Baking sheet**

Sift flour, soda and cream of tartar. Rub in butter until mixture is like fine breadcrumbs. Mix with milk to a soft dough. Roll out and cut in rounds, and put close together on a greased baking sheet. Bake at 230° C, 450° F, Gas 8 for 12 minutes. Cool and pack in sixes or dozens in polythene bags. **Variations** Fruit scones – add 1½ oz sugar and 2 oz dried fruit. Cheese scones – add 3 oz grated cheese and a pinch of salt and pepper. **Thawing and serving** Thaw in wrappings at room temperature for hour, or heat at 180° C, 350° F, Gas for 10 minutes with a covering of foil. **Storage time** 2 months.

Drop Scones or Flapjacks

Self-raising flour	**4 o**
Salt	**1 pinch**
Sugar	**1 o**
Egg	
Milk	**¼ pin**
Margarine, melted	**1 o**

Marmalade

Cooking apples	**½ lb**
Sugar	**1 o**
Lemon juice	**1 tablespoon**
Marmalade	**1 tablespoon**

Sift together the flour, salt and sugar. Add the beaten egg, and then milk. Mix well. Stir in the melted margarine.

Drop the mixture in spoonfuls on a hot griddle, electric hot-plate or frying pan, and cook for 2 minutes on each side. Keep warm in a folded tea-towel while preparing the marmalade.

Peel, core and slice the apples. Simmer gently with the sugar and lemon juice until tender. Stir in the marmalade. Serve hot with the warm pancakes.

Doughnuts **Yield: 16–18 doughnuts**

Lard	**2 o**
Sugar	**2 o**
Egg	
Skim milk powder, made up as liquid	**1 gil**
Plain flour	**8 o**
Salt	**1 pinc**
Baking powder	**2 level teaspoon**
Cinnamon	**½ level teaspoo**
Nutmeg	**¾ level teaspoo**

Cream the lard and sugar. Add the ggs and beat well. Add the milk, then he flour which has been sifted together vith the baking powder and spices. Chill mixture for a short time in a cool arder or a fridge. Put on a lightly oured surface and roll out to $\frac{3}{8}$ inch hickness. Cut with a floured doughnut utter and allow to stand for 15 minutes. ry in deep hot lard 190° C, 375° F, Gas 4 until lightly browned. Turn once uring the cooking process. Drain on bsorbent paper. Dust lightly with ranulated or icing sugar before serving.

pple Loaf

Yield: 6–8 helpings

lain flour, sifted	**1 lb**
alt	**1 pinch**
aking powder	**1 teaspoon**
utter	**4 oz**
ard	**4 oz**
ggs, beaten	**2**
Currants	**2 oz**
Raisins, seeded	**2 oz**
Cooking apple, peeled, cored and sliced	**1**
Milk to mix	
Icing sugar, sifted	**4 oz**
A little water	
Tart eating apple (red), cored and sliced	**1**

Dip the fruit in a little lemon juice as soon as prepared, to prevent discoloration.

Sift together the flour, salt and baking powder. Rub in the fat, mix in the beaten egg, currants, raisins, cooking apple and milk. Mix well. Turn into a 1-lb lined loaf tin, and bake in a moderate oven at 190° C, 375° F, Gas 5 for 40–45 minutes, or until springy and browned. When cool, spread the loaf with a thin icing made with icing sugar and water, and decorate with sliced eating apple. Serve for high tea, especially when salads are scarce.

Drop scones or flapjacks

Index